"Hilarious. . . . Her glass isn't half full—it's 'empty and cracked.'"   —*Entertainment Weekly* (the Must List)

"Razor-sharp."   —*Cosmopolitan*

"A collection of essays in Wentworth's acerbic, bawdy voice. . . . Wentworth makes for great company." —*Elle*

"Wentworth spins hilarious tales of parenting, relationships, and, yes, getting older."   —*People*

"Irresistible. . . . She is sharply observant and incisively funny. . . . Readers who like Nora Ephron and Laurie Notaro won't want to miss Wentworth. Reading this book is like sitting with a best girlfriend—how fitting it is that Wentworth dedicated it to all of hers."

—*Library Journal*

"Wentworth is funny. She gracefully and elegantly bares embarrassing stories from her past and hilariously conveys the challenges of her marriage . . . and of raising their two children. . . . With wit, the author may inspire others to simply enjoy the moment and not let themselves get in the way."   —*Kirkus Reviews*

"Hilarious. . . . The sort of book you'll read through in a single sitting: It's light, laugh out loud, and heartfelt, with plenty of moments that will resonate with women everywhere."   —Gwyneth Paltrow, Goop.com

"An uproariously funny beach read."—*Hamptons* magazine

Happily
Ali
After

ALSO BY ALI WENTWORTH

Ali in Wonderland: And Other Tall Tales

The WASP Cookbook

HARPER

NEW YORK . LONDON . TORONTO . SYDNEY

Happily Ali After

AND OTHER FAIRLY TRUE TALES

Ali Wentworth

HARPER

A hardcover edition of this book was published in 2015 by Harper-Collins Publishers.

HAPPILY ALI AFTER. Copyright © 2015 by Trout the Dog Productions, Inc. All rights reserved. Printed in the United States of America. No part of this book may be used or reproduced in any manner whatsoever without written permission except in the case of brief quotations embodied in critical articles and reviews. For information address HarperCollins Publishers, 195 Broadway, New York, NY 10007.

HarperCollins books may be purchased for educational, business, or sales promotional use. For information please e-mail the Special Markets Department at SPsales@harpercollins.com.

FIRST HARPER PAPERBACK EDITION PUBLISHED 2016.

Designed by William Ruoto

Frontispiece by Heidi Gutman

Library of Congress Cataloging-in-Publication Data has been applied for.

ISBN 978-0-06-223850-4 (pbk.)

16 17 18 19 20   OV/RRD   10 9 8 7 6 5 4 3 2 1

The names and identifying characteristics of some of the individuals featured throughout this book have been changed to protect their privacy. However, if you meet me on the street I will tell you their real names and e-mails.

To all my girlfriends . . .

CONTENTS

· ·

Introduction: The Prime of Miss Ali Wentworth 1

PART I: INSPIRATION

CHAPTER 1   Live and Let Die 9

CHAPTER 2   Opportunity Knocks 21

CHAPTER 3   Set It Free 35

CHAPTER 4   Be Curious 45

CHAPTER 5   That Stinks 57

CHAPTER 6   Greatest Self 67

PART II: MARRIAGE

CHAPTER 7   Grounded 79

· Contents ·

CHAPTER 8   Tug of War 87

CHAPTER 9   Couples Therapy 97

CHAPTER 10   The Other Good Wife. 105

PART III: PARENTING

CHAPTER 11   Not Without My Daughters. 117

CHAPTER 12   Awfully Crabby. 129

CHAPTER 13   Happily Ali After. 139

CHAPTER 14   For You, My Pet. 149

CHAPTER 15   Help! 161

CHAPTER 16   Pool of Regret 169

PART IV: WELLNESS

CHAPTER 17   Move Me 177

CHAPTER 18   Ch-ch-ch-changes 189

CHAPTER 19   Going for the Bronze 197

CHAPTER 20   Not the Face 205

CHAPTER 21   Is That All There Is? 213

CHAPTER 22   Honkers If You
             Like a Good Joke 223

             Acknowledgments 233

Happily
Ali
After

The Prime of Miss
Ali Wentworth

I'm forty-nine years old. God, that hurts. I want to lie, I really do. Please, can't we all shave off a decade? Well, not you teenagers—unless you want to go through puberty again? Now, I know if I were a Pilgrim I would already be dead (their life expectancy in the early 1600s was forty years old). And I have no reason to believe I'll be taken down by scurvy. So, the glass is half full, right? No, the glass is empty and cracked. I'm not concerned about living until I'm a hundred years old; in fact, I'd rather NOT live that long. I don't want to go any deeper on the timeline. I don't want to lose the last few moments of what an elderly person would consider my youth. You see, my prime is behind me and she's laughing at my sagging tush.

How did this happen? Why didn't anyone tell me? I mean, I had a sense about the weather-beaten skin and osteoporosis, but what about the emotional toll? My night sweats are over a loss of bloom, not estrogen depletion. My salad days are over. The greens are wilted and soggy. And who wants leftover salad?

I thought I would delicately leap from forty-nine to fifty the way I have the other stepping-stones of life— with a large slice of bittersweet chocolate cake and some dirty dancing. But not this time. I have lost my balance and fallen into the river of senior despair. Yesterday I peed a little when I laughed.

So now, in my pre-fifty spiral, I decided that instead of succumbing further, I would endeavor to improve myself. I would start training for my second childhood, the winter of my life. And vent. And try to understand exactly what is happening to my abdominal region. This will be difficult because I am losing my memory. Sometimes I stare blankly at one of my daughters because I honestly can't remember what we named her.

But maybe turning fifty is a wake-up call! A chance to stave off decrepitude and better myself in all areas! I know, I'm not going for the gold in gymnastics . . . but I might get out of bed before noon?

When I started writing my last book, I created a Twitter account, as writers are encouraged to do—it is the modern-day way to rise from obscurity and create a fan base (a better fit for me than making a sex tape). I loved the challenge of coining humorous thoughts in 140 characters. (In fact, because I know my editor is reading this: how about we knock this book out in 140 characters and call it a day?) I reveled in the excitement of clicking out my thoughts to the Twittersphere and receiving instant reactions. I now follow everything from @VanillaIce to @BenjaminMoorepaint. Maybe it's because ours is the first generation to have social media. I'm sure it felt the same way in 1876 when the telephone came along: I would have been crank-calling everyone from Grover Cleveland to Sitting Bull. Imagine playing Words with Friends with Emily Dickinson?

A few weeks into my pre-midlife crisis, I stumbled upon an inspirational-quote Twitter feed. I decided to follow it. I'm not that discerning; I also follow @GrilledCheese. The way the feed worked was this: every day at around 9:30 A.M., they sent a single inspirational quote. Now, I grew up in the 1970s when the sayings were very clear and simplistic—"Make love, not war" and "Hang in there, baby"—so at first I felt over-whelmed by some of the deep and intellectual apho-risms. But after a couple of weeks the quotes started to really resonate. They weren't necessarily motivating or goading me, mind you, but rather were making me feel uncomfortably aware that perhaps I wasn't "living life to the fullest." I suddenly felt intense pressure to live a souped-up version of my life based on "Doors of Life" desk calendars and "Sweaty Wisdom" water bottles. What if I did "live today as if it were my last"? Well, I'd be in the Turks and Caicos with a twenty-year-old surfer, a box of Yodels, and a bottle of rosé. No, that sounds superficial and heartless. I would be in Paris with my husband and two daughters. And twenty-year-old surfer—what? I need a babysitter!

The inspirational Twitter feed had me reflecting on my past, as well. I had worked for Oprah Winfrey for a few years as a correspondent and costar on her Friday live show. There was always a "takeaway" from every show and an opportunity for an "aha! moment." And I saw firsthand how virtually every one of her guests was applying the learned spiritual truths to his or her life. One of Oprah's favorite sayings was, "Turn your words into wisdom." But I never said anything that could be remotely construed as enlightened—let alone enlight-ening. I was still treading water under the "Shit hap-pens" slogan.

I didn't want to be spiritually impotent, I realized. I yearned to breathe deep and contemplate more metaphysical matters than the going rate for the tooth fairy or which HP printer was on sale. I'm not an avid churchgoer, Buddhist, Scientologist, or vegan; my gurus are the techie who can fix our WiFi and anyone who can create smoky eyes. A daily inspirational tweet was more my speed. It would be my own spiritual movement. Oprah would be proud. Well, not proud; it takes a lot to make her proud. She's proud of Maya Angelou and Nelson Mandela. But, if all went well, I'd buy some land in upstate New York, a tent, and some chickens, and form a cult.

Now, I realized I faced some obstacles in my path to spiritual enlightenment. I have been accused of being cynical and jaded on this particular subject. I don't read self-help books, except the ones that guarantee I'll lose forty pounds in one hour. And I enjoy being codependent. My best life is never going to resemble, say, Angelina Jolie's; I don't have the cheekbones, can't fly my own plane, and refugees make me too sad. But perhaps I could step up the consciousness a notch.

And while I was at it, why not broaden the quest? I keyed in on the four major food groups of life: spirituality, marriage, parenting, and wellness. Maybe, I thought, as with a car, a lady needed to take herself into the shop for a full overhaul every now and then. Yes, I could use some tinkering under the hood: higher consciousness would definitely give me better road mileage. And exploring marriage would guarantee a cleaner engine and better climate control. Searching for an exceptional navigation system could help steer me through parenting, no? And as for the exterior, well, I wanted a smaller trunk. In other words, I wanted to become Ali 2.0—dynamic, sleeker, and turbocharged. With no money down.

Some might argue that personal growth is a myth—that neither inner nor outer work lasts. But neither do your teeth. Did I emerge from my endeavors a changed person? Yes. Am I thinner? No. Did I decide to start a cult? Well, I have been looking at land in the Catskills. Oprah, you game?

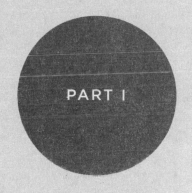

PART I

Inspiration

· ·

YOU CAN'T HAVE EVERYTHING.
WHERE WOULD YOU PUT IT?

—STEVEN WRIGHT

· ·

CHAPTER 1

....

Live and Let Die

TODAY I CHOOSE TO FORGIVE INSTEAD OF HOLDING
ON TO RESENTMENTS. TODAY I CHOOSE TO SEE
EVERYONE WITH THE EYES OF LOVE.

—UNKNOWN

There are very few times in my life when I have truly lived an inspirational quote. And by very few, I mean only once. We can't all be Deepak Chopra, but if we strive for at least one spiritual incentive we may not need Ambien to sleep or chew off nail polish with our teeth. I can't profess to always be able to see people with the eyes of love. Well, maybe John Stamos circa 1992. There have been people I wished unholy harm to—facial disfigurement and genital boils, those sorts of things. I'm not proud of it. But I also don't think I'm alone here; everyone has their pipe dreams. As you're reading this, take stock of the times you considered slashing your boss's tires or putting laxatives in the birthday cake of your diabolical sixth-grade math teacher. In high school did I ponder hiring a prostitute with chlamydia to sip from the same Sprite bottle as the woman who cheated on my father and embezzled all his money? Yes, I did. But I didn't execute it. Mostly because I didn't know how to find a hooker (I hope there's now an app for that) and I had about forty bucks.

But of all the many people who have emotionally harmed me, failed me, or not cast me in a movie of the week, there is one who remained my arch foe for years. I didn't actually know her, but that didn't deter me from eating every crumb of beastly gossip that was handed to me by a third person twice removed.

Daphne was an actress in Los Angeles. Although she and I were the same age, we were different "types"—she was statuesque, brunette, and fetching to my slight, pale, and nonoffensive sex appeal. We didn't run in the same circles. My circle was a bowl of incestuous improv actors who ate their feelings and were encased in insecurity and sexual ambiguity. Daphne's circle was a halo of meticulously scrubbed thespians who were gently kissing success on the lips. On any given weeknight I could be found eating cold enchiladas with my three-legged dog, Racer, while Daphne enjoyed inebriants and giddiness about on-set mishaps with the cast of *Friends*.

And months later she too heard the trumpeting horns of the marching band of fame heading right for her. She was cast in a hit sitcom! You have to understand that being a twenty-year-old actor in L.A. is much like being part of a flock of hungry, begrimed pigeons in the park, and once in a blue moon someone walks by and throws three sunflower seeds. There is a vicious skirmish, an explosion of feathers, and out of the frenzy one bird ascends up to a ranch-style house in the hills with a small infinity pool and their own (leased) BMW and a photo shoot for *InStyle* magazine (back page). The other pigeons yearn for the seed-carrying bird to be decapitated by a telephone wire.

Wait, this story is making me look bad, not Daphne. Did I mention she had big boobs? I suppose that's not an atrocious characteristic. Let's just assume, for the sake of my story, that she bit the heads off kittens. And screamed at babies. The sick ones in the hospital with sad eyes. Orphan babies.

As luck would have it, Daphne worked on a show with my then boyfriend. A writer who, in his youth, went to an all-boys school and would have given a fin ger if someone like the divine Daphne from the Catholic girls' school even looked at him. So there she was with her lithe body prancing on set with her script and her nefarious boobs. Nefarious boobs. Nefarious boobs. Right, I said that. My boyfriend decided to use her as chum in the bloodied waters of my own insecurity. "Daphne is so needy, she's always coming on to me," or "Daphne sleeps with all the writers so she gets a better story line," he would tell me. Well, as a dignified and unemployed actor, I was horrified by the cunning tricks of this minx. She was a slut who bit off kittens' heads! How dare she sully the reputation of all the other refined actresses who were horizontal on casting agents' shag rugs with their legs up in the air, doing their best to gain employment in Hollywood?

I would catch explicit images of her on magazine covers (clutching her exposed breasts with a surprised look as if to say, "I didn't realize there was a crew, hair and makeup, lighting, and a photographer here?"). And walking the red carpet? Well, she did fill out a dress and she was a walking advertisement for doing Tae Bo. But as my mother would say, "She leaves nothing to the imagination!" And I'm not saying that just because she was a teenage model in Paris and I was an overweight gal in gunnysack dresses and jelly sandals.

I broke up with the writer boyfriend for reasons you'll find in my first book, *Ali in Wonderland* (*New*

York Times best-seller, still available on Amazon.com) and rented a bungalow in Santa Monica. Okay, so here's where Daphne radiates in all her deviltry. The day after I left my boyfriend, she showed up at our house (well, now only his house) in a Superman T-shirt WITH-OUT A BRA! Not even twenty-four hours and she drives over to seduce my (once) man who was still face-down on the sofa! She didn't even allow him a grieving period! Plus, everyone knows, you don't pinch a guy whose ex-girlfriend is jealous of you. Yes, I left him . . . but what a strumpet! Even if her intention was to drop by to console a man who was supposedly devastated and impotent, you can't go braless! It's like going commando to sit shiva.

Apparently she was very good at "making him feel better" because within hours they were together every night. And then he took her to the Bahamas. Granted, it was summer and nobody goes to the Bahamas in July, but it was a vacation. And when people vacation to-gether they either return as enemies or hire a wedding planner. This is just my own personal philosophy. When I discovered they were rolling around (hopefully on a nest of sand fleas) together, I had the epiphany that I had made a grave mistake and wanted to reconcile with the writer. I also wanted back in my house. I wanted back in my life. I wanted Daphne gone (gone like *Gone Girl* gone). He took me back, mostly to punish me for leaving him in the first place, and Daphne drove off in her black Lexus. She did leave a silver charm bracelet in a drawer on the bedside table. I threw it in the fire and watched it melt and bubble over a Duraflame log. The dollop of metal is probably still stuck to the side of the hearth.

I moved back into our house (taking care to urinate around the property line) and life went on.

Unfortunately, my rage against the Daphne machine also went on. I mean, I did win! So why was I so fixated on her eradication? The very mention of her name or the word "Newport" (that's where she was born) churned my stomach. Even my closest friends were militarily taught to see her as the enemy. I had gained something I'd only read about in books and seen in James Bond movies: a real nemesis!

I assumed I was as much an antagonist to her. I had thwarted her happiness? Destroyed her life? You know, the shit nemeses do without crushing the person with pythons or using a grenade launcher from a helicopter.

A year later Daphne was getting married to a handsome, athletic, and successful real estate broker. And she was pregnant. This is not the plight of the villain? She was supposed to have her face melt off down to her jawbone or be harpooned under water by a poisonous spear gun! One afternoon I was driving up Coldwater Canyon and screeched to a halt moments before hitting a woman in her forest green sweats and scruffy ponytail. It was Daphne. And she looked blissful hiking with her virile husband and panting dogs. I realized the irony of almost running her over. And more important, of how fast I would be whisked off to prison after my friends' anemic defenses betrayed me on the stand with, "She always hated Daphne! I'm surprised it didn't happen sooner! I think Ali even had an unregistered gun!"

Years later, I was married with babies and living in D.C. I'm not proud of all this preceding disclosure, but I do it in the name of a life lesson I'm providing for you the reader. Occasionally I would catch Daphne on a talk show or in a home magazine, showing off a captivating, classic, spacious, light-filled two-story home with an adjoining stone patio surrounded by a bucolic perennial garden. The ten-foot ceilings boasted a formal powder room, a grand dining room with a subsequent butler's pantry for staging gracious entertaining, a state-of-the-art gourmet eat-in kitchen, and an exquisite master suite with his and hers marble baths complete with sunken tubs. I would badger my husband with photos of her in magazines looking dewy on an exercise bike or flushed on the cover of some pregnancy magazine and I would say to him, "She's so weird looking! Isn't she weird looking?" To which he would have to reply robotically,

"Why yes, honey, she is weird looking." Never once looking up from his book, *Lyndon B. Johnson and the Transformation of American Politics*.

If you, dear reader, have never experienced those feelings or had similar appalling fixations, please keep reading! I redeem myself in the end!

My aha! moment struck one spring afternoon as I was perfecting the art of the homemade cinnamon bun and watching TV. As a child I was allowed only one hour of TV a week so, consequently, in my adulthood I keep the TV on all the time. Much the same way the children who aren't allowed sugar at their home come over to our house and choke on mini marshmallows and finish all my coffee ice cream. A rerun of a show Daphne was guest-starring on suddenly appeared on the screen and I just stopped (mid twisting dough that began dripping through my fingers) and stared in a way I hadn't since the verdict of the O.J. trial. It suddenly hit me: I loathed that woman with more discipline and determination than I had applied to any other endeavor in my life. And yet I met her maybe twice in my life. Had I fabricated the idea of an evil adversary and projected it on to her? Was I just looking for any prey on which to unleash my venom? She dated a guy I had severed ties with, it's not like she drowned my dog or stole my identity. And it was in this moment that I decided to see Daphne through the eyes of love.

I even took it a step further. I got her e-mail address from a mutual friend and wrote to her. A simple note about how funny and beautiful she was in the show I was watching. I unleashed it into the cyber universe. I didn't need to get a response, the cathartic act was enough. However, after I sent the e-mail, I ate most of the raw dough and took a two-hour nap.

Daphne responded later that day with an innocuous, but kind thank you. An Internet relationship had been sparked. We wrote back and forth for a couple of weeks and when my family scheduled a trip to Los Angeles, Daphne invited us over to her home. This is a huge move in the foreplay of friendship.

The drive to her house was as winding emotionally as the coastal curves we hugged. My husband was profoundly confused, as he had been programmed to detest her and now he was being lectured on how to seem merry and blithe. I kept repeating to him, "Don't say anything about anything," which was as lucid as I could be in that moment.

Keep in mind, this was not one-sided. Daphne told me later she considered me equally psychotic and repugnant. As we careened into her driveway, I had a fleeting sense of what the invasion of Normandy must have felt like, "where ignorant armies clash by night."

If you had been her Chihuahua mix, you'd have thought we were long-lost friends, perhaps even sisters.

Later in the afternoon, she and I took a stroll and exchanged tidbits of gossip we had heard about each other (and chose to believe) and the seething malevolence we harbored. When in your life do you get to face the (former) enemy and say, "I loathed you with such intensity, you skanky whore"? Obviously this excludes anyone going through puberty.

I inquired as to why she felt compelled to cruise over to my house—braless no less!—the second my car was out of the driveway! Daphne laughed hysterically. "I don't own a Superman T-shirt and I never go braless; my boobs are uneven!" (A couple of months later Daphne sent me a Superman T-shirt in the mail that I still wear.) I changed tactics and peppered her with questions like, "How could you go to the Bahamas with him?" She answered coolly, "I was the one going, he followed me! He didn't spend a dime on me." Okay, okay . . . "Why leave your silver charm bracelet in the bedside table for me to find?" She looked confused, and said, "I don't wear silver; it didn't belong to me!" And, with the feeling of an EpiPen being jabbed in my thigh, I remembered that the bracelet was actually mine! It was given to me at my high school graduation and I put it away because the charms kept scratching my wrist. Oh my God! I melted my own jewelry!

Daphne had invited her only other Greek friend to

be padding for the afternoon in case things got out of hand. Did she envision a chicken fight? Each of us on the shoulders of a Greek, like in a chariot race? While the two of us walked on the beach and exhaled all of our festering resentments, my husband and the Greek friend talked about the Los Angeles Saint Sophia Greek Orthodox Cathedral renovation and what town their grandparents were born in (on the off chance they might be related, as all Greek people believe they are). And, like burning a bundle of sage, the demons evaporated.

Daphne is now one of my closest friends. Our families spend summers together. I've taught her children to paint clamshells and they have taught us the art of boogie boarding and how to eat macro greens. I know all of Daphne's secrets. I know what irritates her (and the list is long). I know when she's ready to leave a party just by a raised eyebrow. I know her shoe size and the name of her dermatologist. I've seen her naked physically and emotionally. I know the names of every boy she's ever kissed. Again the list is long. I know what her fears are. I know what her dreams are.

I'm often nostalgic about the period of my life when I had a nemesis, but I would trade the knotted stomach and heinous thoughts for this enlightened friendship any day. I can't say I see EVERYONE through the eyes

of love now. Steady on. I mean, if you steal my parking space, I'm going to flip you the bird. But I won't
fantasize about lowering you into reactor coolant and
watching you boil to death. Live and let live, that's my
new motto.

CHAPTER 2

· ·

Opportunity Knocks

WHENEVER OPPORTUNITY KNOCKS,

ANSWER THE DOOR.

—ANONYMOUS

I have heard this oldie but goodie put in a variety of
ways—if opportunity rings, answer it, if opportunity
Facebooks, friend it, if someone hands you their purse,
take it . . . you get the drift.

I wholeheartedly embrace this sentiment. We spend
most of our lives beseeching the higher powers for fortu-
itous circumstances, and when they materialize, we should

take advantage of them. Most of the time it's fear, overly cautious parents, or jealous lovers that thwart us from embracing opportunity. And yet sometimes, just sometimes, we don't think through what the opportunity entails. We jump at the idea of it, like a dolphin to a mackerel at Sea-World, but don't truly ponder the weight of the task.

I get excited whenever I'm offered anything, whether it's a sample of Pinkberry frozen yogurt, a goody bag, or a job. The best part of receiving any offer for which you're getting paid (bonus!) is the offer itself, not the actual labor that it entails. And, my husband will attest, I have a tendency to lack comprehension when I'm offered a career opportunity. I'm not meticulous. I miss things like "shoots in Poland" or "nudity required." Usually what transpires is the day before the job starts, I cry, have a panic attack (heavy breathing like there's a serial killer calling me from inside the house), and try to invent a persuasive reason why I can't fulfill the contract. Evidence has shown that any excuse that involves lady parts always earns you a free pass. The mere mention of the word "vagina" can silence any institution, studio, or corporation. And they will never press you for details.

I was in my kitchen on a stormy afternoon making chocolate chip cookies with my daughters (the trick is sea salt and Ghirardelli semisweet chips). Well, making the dough. We like to eat it frozen. With forks. Late at night. After we've brushed our teeth. My agent called to tell me I had been offered a job doing a commencement speech, which was very lucrative, and they would fly me to the university and home on a private plane. Well, I almost choked on the gigantic glob of brown sugar I had just shoved in my mouth. The commencement was for a large university in the Midwest. We will call it Western Missouri University (unless there really is a Western Missouri University, in which case we'll call it Midwest State). I didn't catch the name, but did catch the amount. It was months away, so I put it in my calendar and went back to wrapping globs of dough in parchment paper and freezer bags. I was so blown away that anyone would ask me to address an honorable academic establishment, I figured I was ready to announce the silent auction at my daughter's elementary school!

Two weeks before the graduation date, I received a detailed e-mail about my travel and the itinerary. The first question was what snacks I required for the plane ride. That's right, I was going on a private jet like Beyoncé and Donald Trump. And I could hand-pick the snacks? What would Katy Perry pick? If I asked for lobster tails and cotton candy, would that seem presumptuous? How about a smorgasbord of cold meats and French cheeses? No, I would be modest and demure and request just some chili-cheese fries, a couple of Cronuts, mint

Milanos, and a six-pack of Canada Dry ginger ale. I took a moment to fantasize about reclining in the beige leather Gulf Stream La-Z-Boy chair and holding up my flute for more ginger bubbly. I'd be wearing a purple velour and diamond-bejeweled tracksuit, turban, and dark Jackie O sunglasses. A petite Ukrainian woman would paint my nails while I perused the pages of Italian *Vogue*. Yes, in my fantasy I'm a Real Housewife of Bulgaria. And then I read farther down the schedule . . .

My speech was scheduled for 9 A.M., 1:30 P.M., and 5 P.M. This made no sense. It must have been a typo; how could I deliver one commencement speech three times? My husband, using the voice he had used when toilet training our daughters, informed me that large universities have to divide up their student body and, therefore, I was giving the speech three different times to three different factions of the school. And then he broke into a fit of laughter. (Well, the laugh was on him because I was the one who finished his beloved peanut butter that day after he went to work.) I couldn't fathom a scenario in which I made a speech three times in one day. I mean, even Stalin didn't make three speeches in one day. And he had a very strong mission statement!

I don't have a fear of flying except for when the cabin loses pressure, the plane spirals, and the stewardesses hit the floor screaming, "We're all going to die!" And even then I can usually nap through it. I've never considered the possibility of my life ending in such a dramatic way; I assume my demise will come in the form of choking on a chicken wing splinter while lying sideways on the couch watching *Veep*. But on the afternoon I was meant to travel, there were horrible thunderstorms in the Midwest. My husband was concerned for my safety and thought I should fly commercial (with a layover), rent a car, and drive the rest of the four hours. Are you kidding me? The whole reason I accepted this gig was to fly on a private plane! And no lightning storm would stop me. If I was going to disappear without a trace, then I would do so on a Bombardier Challenger 300.

The entire drive from my apartment to the airport in New Jersey was like being trapped in a never-ending car wash. The storm was worse than reported, so threatening and menacing that it was even given a name: Andrea. And whenever the weather channel refers to an impending climate calamity by name, you know it is monumental. (I hope they never have to resort to names like Boo, Wiggles, or Doodle Bug.) The taxi drove right onto the tarmac. There was no endless security line behind the woman who can't fold the baby stroller or the absentminded guy who forgot to take off his belt and then adds coin after coin to the plastic bowl. But there was no magazine stand either, so no Big Red gum or *Cosmo*'s "Eight sexy things to do with your toes." At least when you fly Jet Blue you can enjoy the food court. I find it stressful to fly without inhaling some Panda Express Beijing beef and an Auntie Anne's bucket of cinnamon-sugar pretzel nuggets.

I leaped out of the car and into a subterranean rain puddle. A nice airport employee wrapped in neon yellow rubber sheets escorted me up the rickety steps to the aircraft. It was the size of a toy plane that toddlers with glue and enamel paint assembled. My tiny ship on the Peter Pan ride in Disney World had more leg room. It also smelled like urine, which is not an unfamiliar scent because I do live with two incontinent dachshunds. I couldn't stand up straight because of the low ceilings and I noticed my air vent was duct-taped shut. It was not the billionaires' boys' club vessel I had envisioned. I hoped, based on the two propellers, that we might slow down and do some crop dusting as we headed west across God's country. I also prayed the plane registered more aerospace technology than the rope and brick used as the brakes. I thought about Amelia Earhart; I wondered what she had packed for snacks. And if her plane had two propellers.

After what seemed like days (I was the tiny dot that arrows across the world map from India and up through Asia in an Indiana Jones movie), I heard the deafening screech of the wheels being lowered. Were we airdropping some cornmeal over Somalia? I could barely make out the chalky runway in the middle of a potato field. The plane skidded and wobbled and finally shuddered to a stop. One of the pocket pilots climbed down and fastened the brick and rope brake around the plane wheels. As I walked across the basketball court of an airfield, I noticed there wasn't another human in sight. Not even any children of the corn. My Google map informed me that the town I was in could not be found. I was un-Googleable.

My motel room overlooked a grim parking lot of four-wheelers and junkers. In the middle of the night, I was awakened by a couple of inebriated truckers screaming about how they "couldn't find pussy"! I was too nervous about my commencement speech the next day to volunteer. And I sympathized with them; I was just as frustrated because I couldn't find the TV remote. Finally, the chicken haulers were gone. They must have lucked out and found what they were looking for. But just as one fire is put out, another pops up. Whenever the family (of what sounded like seventeen) in the next room flushed the toilet, my whole room shook. It didn't shake like someone walking in Timberlake work boots, it shook like the Amtrak Acela had derailed and was heading toward my queen-size bed with the stained headboard. I abandoned sleep and instead concocted a late-night snack of stale Lorna Doones and Lay's potato chips from the hallway vending machine and watched the early, early local news, the early local news, and then the local news. I sure hope they finally caught that bear!

I skipped the free all-you-can-eat waffle, eggs, sausage, and grits breakfast and headed to the university. I had bought a demure, yet flirty Tory Burch dress and pink pumps, forgetting I would be covered in a heavy robe and itchy cap all day. Even the uncomfortable hosiery that cut off all circulation in my thighs was wasted. When I arrived I was escorted to a room packed with faculty clutching their Dunkin' Donuts coffee cups and the president (of the university, don't get excited) preparing for the event. They all wore comfortable khaki slacks and Merrill shoes (sensible walking shoes that people from Palo Alto wear). I felt like a hooker at a global environment initiative summit. We lined up in two straight lines and began a procession down many hallways and stairs. Stumbling in my heels, I had to be rescued by the ethics professor more than once. When the pomp and circumstance music began, we triumphantly marched into the stadium like we were ready to invade Lebanon!

I sat up on the stage in a regal-looking chair feeling like a complete fraud. I was a B-minus student on a good day (not including art and free play) and here I was taking up space usually allotted for people who discovered cures to infectious diseases and the woman who invented Spanx. Let's be clear, I was not getting a doctorate or an honorary degree, but I was wearing the same costume as the theoretical physicist, the recipient of a big bronze medallion, next to me. And being the headliner in a stadium where I was not going to fly down on a harness like Pink made me fidgety. It was all about my words. I had to inspire! I had to be a spiritual guide to those young adults who were mostly hungover and taking selfies. I was like John Kennedy, Winston Churchill, and Oprah, poised to bestow wisdom and values. And it would probably be recorded. I felt a rush of nausea. The masses and the royal court onstage stood, hands on our hearts, and sang "The Star-Spangled Banner." I was hoping nobody noticed when I mumbled through "twilight's last gleaming." Streaming? The president of the university orated about community and new beginnings, the smarty-pants next to me received his award, and then I was introduced. I wasn't as panicked as I was the first time I did *The Tonight Show.* My knees weren't buckling and I wasn't seconds from blacking out on Keanu Reeves's lap. But as I approached the podium and caught a glimpse of the throng of faces assembled in the sports arena, it struck me that at that precise moment I needed to be more Martin Luther King and less Andrew Dice Clay. I had to make an impact. People remember their commencements! I needed to quote Steve Jobs and rally them to do great things like creating self-healing mutating cells or eradicating lines at airport security. I think wearing the robe really threw me. I felt like Peter Dinklage in *Game of Thrones*.

I'm not saying my speech will go down in history on a par with "I have a dream" or "Ask what you can do for your country," but it was authentic and got some yucks. My message was to find laughter and humor in life. (If you send me a self-addressed stamped envelope and a money order for two dollars, I'll send you the speech. No, not really.) Yes, there was rousing applause at the end.

I sat back down confident and fatigued. Adrenaline is a curious neurotransmitter because it fuels you with energy—like the first inhale of the crack pipe, I assume—and then the withdrawal is utter exhaustion. It's not dissimilar to childbirth, except you can't be on drugs. But nothing prepared me for the debilitation of watching hundreds of students line up, cross the stage with frozen smiles, and receive their diplomas. Over and over and over again. I clapped for the first two hundred, but to avoid bleeding palms, nodded to the rest. I passed the remaining hour fixated on shoes. I never realized how much you could tell about a person's character solely based on their footwear. And I never realized how disgusted I am by men who wear sandals and don't wash. (My speech should have incorporated the sage advice that Birkenstocks plus toe fungus will never get you employed or laid.) There were more bejeweled stilettos than a Vegas stripper convention. I quietly hoped a girl would go tumbling down the stairs. Mean, I know, but I was so bored.

Finally, the commencement was over. The procession careened through the crowd and back into the main building. Ordinarily this would be the part of the day when the commencement speaker shakes a lot of alumni hands, grabs a Diet Dr Pepper, and makes haste to a waiting car. But no! I had two more "shows." Lord Jesus, I needed oratory Viagra.

I decided that with the 1:30 speech I would shift some stories around, perhaps add a made-up prison tale to shake things up (scare them straight). I was getting more at ease with my platform, and the chafing robe had started to wear my scent. In the same way stand-ups work out new material at the Comic Strip, I would use Western Missouri University as my incubator.

In between gigs, I secluded myself in a frigid football conference room. There was a dry-erase board with old plays written out in red pen and, flung under the table, a knee brace that looked like it had been mauled by pit bulls. And it stank like pickled feet. The room would have been a decent place to hide and purchase my kids' school clothes on oldnavy.com but for the sensor-activated lighting. Midway through placing my order for "polka dot cozy socks," the room abruptly went pitch-black. I scrimmaged like an insane person and jumped up and down until the halogens were once again ablaze.

I sheepishly entered the faculty lounge where the lighting was constant. And discussed the weather. Local weather. National weather. Weather changes. Whether there'd be weather. Until the professor of agriculture told us it was, once again, time to line up. We promenaded down the hallways and staircases and stopped just outside the stadium doors. I was in my own version of *Groundhog Day*.

Speech number two was sharper and improved. I paused more, allowed the words to resonate, and added funny faces. Welcome to the Improv, ladies and gentlemen!

After the applause, I sat down to face the relentless parade of more diplomas and hairy toes. They should punish terrorists by shackling them to metal fold-out chairs and making them witness every graduation at Arizona State (largest public university enrollment in 2014 of 60,168).

By this point, I had become a fixture on campus, like the local bartender or the senior pot dealer. I could have had my own office, hell, my own building, and ALI IS OUR SPIRIT ANIMAL sweatshirts. I knew the faculty by their first names, "Bob, are you gonna finish that key lime pie?" The hour before the third speech was spent analyzing a persnickety business professor who believed her husband was being unfaithful. The fact that he never made it home before dawn because he continually "fell asleep" at his desk or had massive amounts of papers to grade were, to me, blazing signs of infidelity. But it was not my business to get emotionally involved (our sisterhood would expire in three hours), so I shrugged and proclaimed, "Educating is exhausting business. I say let him sleep in his office if he wants. But you're right, not on Christmas Eve." But inside I wanted to say, "Girlfriend, your husband is probably bedding everything in a cashmere button-down and wool skirt; hire a lawyer and hide your valuables, it's about to get real!"

Thirty minutes later, we were marching out AGAIN to the clanging of the school band cymbals. I was borderline delirious and thought about all the scientific studies that have been done about physical exhaustion and how you can literally go crazy. I didn't want to be taken away in a straitjacket to the Missouri State Mental Institute. The one in Palm Beach, maybe. My third and final commencement speech was a blur, like doing karaoke drunk—or for me, doing karaoke sober. I vaguely recall huge applause, so I knew it went well, and my clothes were still on, which was a good sign.

They should have taken me to the airport on a gurney. I'd felt like this once before when I was being carted into the operating room and they had just injected a "calming" potion into my IV. The only difference was that I didn't sing "my milkshake brings all the boys to the yard" through the intensive-care ward.

I curled up in the Barbie plane, as frail as the tubercular Fantine in *Les Miz*, the words of my speech repeating over and over in my head. If someone had prodded me with a stick, I would instinctively have stood up and recited a fourth commencement speech.

The next day I slept for sixteen hours. And got a vitamin B shot. I knew from then on that when opportunity knocked, I would open the door chastely, read the fine print, Google the location, and remind myself that 40 percent of the paycheck goes to taxes.

And as I lay in bed sipping my kale-apple-ginger smoothie I remembered the president of the university putting her arm around me and saying, "Thank you so much for doing this! You know we can never get ANYONE to do our commencement!" Well, small wonder. At least when you climb Kilimanjaro, you do it once.

CHAPTER 3

· ·

Set It Free

IF YOU LOVE SOMETHING, SET IT FREE. IF IT COMES
BACK IT'S YOURS, IF IT DOESN'T, IT NEVER WAS.
—RICHARD BACH

I don't know who Richard Bach was, but I think he was extremely misguided. If I set everything I loved free, I would end up with a can of anchovy paste and some XXL turtlenecks given to me many Christmases ago by my mother, who purchased them at an outlet in Vermont. Although if I did let those turtlenecks free, they would definitely find their way back to me. They have been donated to charity many times over, but miraculously always appear back in my closet.

And why, if I love something, should I give it away in the first place? I'm not a Buddhist, I don't renounce materialism, but I'm not Mariah Carey with a multimillion-dollar shoe fetish either. Some things I just don't want to let go of. And that goes for people as well. Should I have done this with both my children? I love my babies! But if I had swaddled them in fluffy baby blankets and placed them in a box from the Container Store with a bunny soother and a bottle of formula and set them adrift on the Hudson River, I'm positive they would not have come back to me. I'd be in Bellevue strapped to a gurney with a Popsicle stick in my mouth. And I would have to confess that the evil voices in my head didn't make me do it, but Richard Bach, a twentieth-century writer with a passion for aeronautics. But, I suspect I'm probably being too literal here.

Love is an ethereal thing and cannot be owned and cannot be taken. And if it goes away, then it was never meant to be, but if it comes back then it's true love. Well, if it's true love, then why did he leave in the first place? If you set him free, he gets to screw around and then decide whether or not to come back, and if he does decide to come crawling back, then why would you want him? To set free implies he's been imprisoned, enslaved, and, therefore, probably really pissed. And, anyway, in the most optimistic scenario, if he does come back to you, he's probably riddled with STDs.

When Kathy Bates tied James Caan to the bed in *Misery,* it was very clear the intent was not to set him free. And she knew that if she did release him, he would go to the authorities, or kill her. So she did the right thing! Well, except he did ultimately kill her.

Leo was majestic and imposing and smelled like warm vanilla. It was the only time in my life, aside from with my husband, that I experienced a true carnal appetite. Leo was a Portland-based photographer who came to Los Angeles on a temporary film job. It was clear by his swagger that he was single. And he had tattoos—the true branding of a bad boy. But also perfect teeth—a combo as rare as an albino Amur leopard.

At that time in my life, I compromised when it came to relationships. I would overlook fundamental issues like fidelity, alcoholism, and a propensity toward sex with men. I was so dazzled with Leo. (Even though I knew deep down that any long-term relationship with him would entail my solitary breastfeeding of a colicky baby while receiving texts and photos of him with topless ingénues in St. Barth's. "I'm a photographer, honey, this is work! The girls have to be naked and sprinkled with white sand. And the champagne is only to loosen them up"!)

It's amazing how a man's scent can narcotize a woman into a spell of complete abandon and recklessness. Yes, just like what all perfume ads say.

After months of serving as a Protestant geisha to his mercurial affections, I had to face the fact that it was time for Leo to return to Oregon. Yes, our relationship had a shelf life. I refused to be the emotionally indigent woman begging for an engagement ring or a vial of his blood, or accost him with a fake pregnancy scare. (I have known male friends who were harnessed with the girl-friend who flushed the pill down the toilet or punctured holes in the condoms and presented pregnancy like it was a freshly baked pie as he had one foot out the door. This never unfolds happily. It's a sure recipe for ending up a single mother, except with even more rage and a smaller net in the dating pool.)

With Leo, I decided to be detached and aloof, yet still seductive and freshly waxed. The clichéd aforementioned phrase, "If you love something, set it free. If it comes back it's yours, if it doesn't, it never was," echoed in my head, inevitably merging into the Police lyric, "If you love someone set them free . . . free, free, set them free." I decided the only way to ensure his coming back was to make it impossible for him to leave in the first place. (See: the aforementioned *Misery*.)

I couldn't rely on my less than stellar sexual techniques or my feeble bank account. And then it came to me, the same way it came to that psychotic female astronaut who decided to wear Depends while she drove across the country. I would take Leo to Hawaii for the weekend as our final soirée before he departed for Oregon. A romantic tropical dream that he would never want to wake from, certainly not to move back to windswept, rainy Oregon with all those moose. Or mooses. Meese?

I borrowed some money from my friend who had a safeguarded corporate job and an actual savings account. I found that if I could sustain a balance of zero at the end of every month, then I was ahead of my financial curve, which always careened downward. Obviously, the fact that my friend had tons of leftover coin meant it was free for the taking, up for grabs; she could have just burnt it in her balcony hibachi.

Leo was having lunch with a business acquaintance at a trendy Italian eatery, Locanda Veneta, in Beverly Hills. I knew that because I would scour his itinerary late at night after he succumbed to a two-bottle-of-Merlot stupor. Okay, stop judging, everyone has gone through their boyfriend's private agenda or iPhone, right?

I felt I needed the element of surprise so Leo would not have much time to consider or reconsider the offer. I had a letter placed on his table before Leo and his lunch mate were seated. I had run out to the Paper Source, where you can buy recycled cards that smell like sweet sage for eight dollars. And in my amateurish calligraphy scripted a *Downton Abbey*–type invitation for the weekend away at a secret location. The bottom stated, "Nothing to pack, bathing suit optional." I had become the siren of amour. I knew subconsciously I was wasting my craftiness on the wrong person, but I have a tendency to get enraptured in whatever life fantasy I'm performing at that moment. Sometimes I sing "Don't Cry for Me, Argentina" out our apartment window wearing a feather boa. Doesn't bother me that children point and laugh.

Leo had no inkling as to our covert destination even after we taxied down the runway. Just as the wheels went up, the stewardess, in her saccharine way, belted out, "Aloha!" Leo turned to me and said, "We're going to Japan?" He was from rural Oregon.

We stayed in one of six clusters of thatched-roof huts on the Kohala Coast. The rooms featured a four-poster bed with Hawaiian flowers carved into it, an outside rain shower, nightly baths with floating orchids and candles. And the breakfast buffet? As many *malasadas* (Portuguese doughnuts deep fried and coated with sugar), pancakes with macadamia nut sauce, kalua pig sausages, Spam (Hawaii is the largest consumer of Spam in the world) you can pile on your plate, and fresh papaya juice. He was Tarzan, me Jane. He actually looked like Tarzan . . . I was more Jane . . . but fully clothed

and wearing sunblock. Our days were filled with splash-
ing in the luminous sea, dancing at luaus of suckling pig
with quaint local Hawaiian ukulele bands who belted
out "La Bamba" and "Like a Virgin." Yes, the sand was
black and gravelly and every dish I ordered had a shrimp
tail sticking out of it (and this includes desserts), but I
had isolated Leo from his known and familiar habitat. I
had immersed him in a trans-Pacific Zen sanctuary of
geothermal wonders and wicker chairs. And as it turned
out, he's one of the few Oregonians able to take the sun;
he browned instead of appearing like he had just come
from a chemical peel. I really knew I loved him when I
discovered he didn't wear open-toe sandals.

One afternoon we strolled down to the shore to the
exclusive Four Seasons for lunch. We consumed four
mango mojitos (well, he did, I had a sip), some spicy ahi
poke, coconut crab cakes, washimi Kobe beef skewers,
and polenta-fried calamari. The Four Seasons in Hawaii
is a second home to many of the studio brass in Hollywood. So naturally, I charged our lunch to an executive
who once tried to feel me up. I only hazarded a guess he
was staying there, but, as with most clichéd Hollywood
hunches (hair plugs) I was right and we got a free meal.

Confident that a weekend by the sea and verdant,
lush flora would deter Leo from the miserably rain-
sodden and unshaven bevy of mountaineer women, I
flew back to Los Angeles rosy and buoyant.

The day after homeward-bound Leo left for the airport, I spent the entire day in bed. Well, first I made myself a goat cheese omelet and downed a box of Raisinets. I still held on to the notion that he would realize his mistake, grab a fistful of blueberries (isn't that what Oregon is known for?), and board the first Southwest Airlines flight back to Los Angeles. In other words, after all the setting-free business, he would come back to me. When I saw in what turmoil he'd left the bathroom (half-used shaving cream, toothpaste smeared all over the sink, shower drain clogged with dark hair), it did anesthetize the sting a bit.

But he never did come back to me. There were no naked frolicking ingénues, no torrid affair with Swedish models. He ended up marrying a lovely physical therapist and had six children. And appears very happy. He probably even changes dirty diapers.

Wait, this story doesn't end so simplistically; it's not a tear-jerker. I wouldn't have written this tale if it didn't come out smelling like the leis that hung around my neck in the Waikiki airport.

When I set Leo free, something else came back to me. Something better . . .

Leo took a book to Hawaii, which I found slightly offensive, as I assumed the weekend would be spent gazing into each other's eyes and stimulating dirty parts.

I mean, I was going away for an erotic adventure, not Oprah's book club! The best-seller he purchased was a memoir of life in the White House. Why that and not *Lady Chatterley's Lover*? I'd have settled for *The Joy of Sex* (I actually had some questions about a couple of things). But Leo was obsessed with politics, a subject that I had come to loathe as a result of my upbringing in D.C. submerged in all the minutiae of the Nixon administration.

Leo would lie out on a sun chaise with his simian features and glistening tattoos as he read excerpts from the book aloud to me. "'From my chair pushed up against the President's desk, I was the link between Clinton and the House Democrats'"—"Fascinating!" he would then bellow. I would lie next to him (eyes rolling) perusing *People* magazine and scrolling through the best and worst bodies in Hollywood. I found myself competing with this political confidant Leo kept quoting. As I would rub sunscreen on Leo's toned thighs, I would hear (ad nauseam) about Colin Powell's foreign-aid policies. Eventually I snapped. "Jesus! Can you stop quoting George Stephanopoulos for five minutes so we can get it on!"

Leo's infatuation with the book lasted for all three days we were in Hawaii. I would sheepishly hide it under his towel when I emerged from the ocean in my snorkel gear carrying a handful of cowrie shells or toss it into the laundry bag at night. But, magically, the book would appear in his hands again by sunrise.

Leo left the book on my bedside table the day he disappeared from my life. As well as some loose change and an unfinished prescription bottle of codeine. And that same battered paperback with mai tai stains sits on my office shelf today.

I married George Stephanopoulos, author of the memoir that foiled my passion play on the isle of Maui. I loved something, set it free, and something even better came back to me. And I'm never setting George free. I don't care what Sting says.

CHAPTER 4

....

Be Curious

BE CURIOUS, NOT JUDGMENTAL.

—WALT WHITMAN

It's impossible to live in our society with an open heart and an open mind (and closed legs). I am bombarded by the Internet, on TV, at potlucks, by the brutal snap judgments people make about everyone else! I'm not proud to say that I fall prey to it. Just for an example: I hate Kendall Jenner. I don't even know Kendall Jenner. I wouldn't know Kendall Jenner if she knocked on my door and said, "Hi! I'm

Kendall Jenner!" But I hate Kendall Jenner. Why? I guess because I'm supposed to?

It's easy to look down on all the haters on the Internet who harsh on (anonymously) the general population, but you don't have to be a forty-seven-year-old recluse who lives over his parents' garage and downloads porn all day to pass vicious judgment on a daily basis. Of course, trolls (and I'm talking the trash-talking kind, not the creepy ones who frequent chat rooms dedicated to dungeons) offer the most flagrant examples of ignorant vitriol; they don't try to understand, accept, or even know the people they so swiftly condemn. And if I ever did bump into @DirtyPieHole on the street, I'm sure he would be very sweet and gracious, unlike his comments: "If Ali has cancer, then sorry, but she is one ugly bitch #WearMakeup." I would forgive him only if he was actually missing a face.

But let's be honest: we all judge others, usually without making the slightest attempt to address the fact that our judgment is born of ignorance. And as a guy I dated from Brown who dropped a lot of acid once said, "You have to have understanding to have acceptance and then love." He also totaled my Saab.

Now that I am in my forties, I aim to be more accepting. Unless you're a man wearing knee-length denim

shorts. Or have a goatee. Or use #grateful on your
Twitter feed. Oh God, I'm doing it. Okay. Open heart.

I was recently at a fiftieth (she says forty-seventh)
birthday party in Malibu, California. A place famous
for being incredibly judgy, but in a non judgy way. "It's
all good" is the cornerstone of the vernacular on Point
Dume, yet it is only "all good" if you're Pilates fit, surf,
have a Frank Gehry beach shack, and are sleeping with
your yoga instructor. Malibu is also one of the few places
in the world where you pay hundreds of dollars for worn
and tattered sweatshirts. Fine, I bought two. But in my
defense, I was on Ambien because of jet lag. I also have
no recollection of purchasing six pairs of the exact same
jeans on that drug. (My friend Amelia took an Ambien
and bought five princess canopy beds from a Pottery
Barn kids' catalog. She doesn't have children.)

The birthday party was made up of a group of eight
women, some of us who knew each other, others who
were meeting for the first time. It's was a real girls' night
with an ocean view and a delicious board of smelly
French cheeses and bottles of Pouilly-Fuissé. We were
all exuberant to be away from kids and husbands for a
night of debauchery (which for women my age meant
a night of delving into such topics as varicose veins, sex
dreams about the contractor, and the latest pill everyone
was taking for anxiety). All topped off with some form
of dark chocolate.

As a surprise, one of the women had invited a psychic to perform, and I mean perform, after dinner. Well, how could I not roll my eyes? I'd seen enough *20/20* episodes on fraud to know how these spiritual translators work. "Are you kidding me? Isn't there an Argentinean masseuse or someone who creates henna tattoos available?" (It was Malibu, after all.) I mean, really: a *psychic*?

I assumed my outburst would be met with a resounding, "Yeah, she's right, this is stupid! Let's watch the *Orange Is the New Black* marathon!" But instead I was reprimanded with a lecture on how amazing she was and how most of the women frequented psychics. Turns out, as often as Greeks do electrolysis. It was at this moment I had to breathe deep and recall the wise words of Walt Whitman. I was in Malibu; I would be receptive to new possibilities. I would shed my narrow-minded, dogmatic approach like the Patagonia jacket I arrived in.

A glass of wine and a hunk of Camembert later, the psychic arrived. Her name was Donna. Now, what psychic is named Donna? Clear my mind, breathe, and find ethereal attunement . . .

Donna wore a long, black, sexy Jersey beach dress with a plunging neckline. I guess she hadn't read the e-mail about it being all women. But if she was psychic, wouldn't she have *known*? We all sat in a circle on what felt like a Moroccan rug made of baby llamas. There was a fire roaring and the scent of freesia/fig candles wafting through the room. All the cell phones were turned off as well as Coldplay strumming from the iPod; Donna had our full attention.

I'm not saying a psychic should have an undetectable exotic accent, but Donna was straight out of Staten Island. I banished the thought from my brain; psychics aren't from one mystic island, Ali. Surely somewhere in Carson City, Nevada, or Rancho Cucamonga there were clairvoyants being born by the minute.

Steady on.

If Donna were a stand-up, she would have been heckled off in the first minute. "I'm sensing women . . . Americans . . ." My nine-year-old could have done better. And has. She once predicted that, based on the tampons and Aleve I was buying, Mommy would lose her temper at some point during that day. And she was correct. Donna looked at my friend Lizzy, who is svelte and stunningly beautiful in a Swedish kind of way. "You had a grandmother?" Donna asked. The fact that Lizzy exists is a pretty stellar indication that she had a grandmother. "I see your grandmother . . . she was a very beautiful woman . . . tall." I took some deep breaths. What gave it away, the fact that Lizzy could rest her wineglass on Gisele Bündchen's head?

After a series of common observations about dead people that none of us could dispute—who knows if one's great-grandfather regretted his life? Or if an eighteenth-century aunt missed her childhood home?— Donna moved on to Polly. "I see a dog?" Polly nodded. I mean, chances are at some point in our lives we have all come across, owned, or even petted a dog. "A white, fluffy dog." Polly shook her head. "A medium-size dog? Black?" Polly shook her head again. After we exhausted the probability of whether the dog was a Jack Russell or a Great Dane, Polly, who was so deflated from having to tell Donna she was wrong, finally lied and confirmed that yes, it was a bulldog. Donna smiled with pride, one breast slipping out the side of her urban muumuu.

After an hour of watching Donna close her eyes, pace the floor, and wait for spiritual signs (all of which was as riveting as C-Span coverage of Congressional budget hearings), we all took an intermission to fetch wine, rifle through the fridge, and check e-mails. Donna circled like a shark, presumably on the hunt for psychic clues. And then disappeared into the ladies' room (you don't have to be psychic to know when to pee).

Finally, I was up at supersensory bat. Donna stared at me like she was discerning whether I was a real diamond or cubic zirconium. "I'm getting images of a book?" I nodded. "Funny . . . a funny manuscript?" I nodded again. "I'm feeling big things, big success . . ." Like a fly to poisonous sticky paper, my ego clung to every word. Yes, yes . . . more, more . . . Who was I to decide if there are forces not recognized by natural laws out there? I had no evidence either way, and Patricia Arquette was so convincing in *Medium*. Maybe Donna did have second sight? I stared into her eyes with razor focus, like a samurai preparing for battle. I wanted more. Would a studio option my book? Would Reese Witherspoon play me?

Clearly exhausted, Donna moved on to Ashley. Damn, just when I was about to ask her if she could visualize me on Jay-Z's yacht. While Ashley tried to recall whether she had golden retrievers growing up, I hatched a plan. I would fly to Los Angeles once a month for readings, and when I was prevented from coming because of stomach flu or parent-teacher conferences, perhaps I could Skype? I'm really not a fan of phone sessions. When I left Los Angeles years ago, the two things I missed most were inexpensive avocados and my shrink. I would erratically book phone sessions, but became increasingly distraught when I heard what sounded like frying or maybe a hair dryer in the background. No matter. I would find a way.

My reverie was interrupted as Tina, the birthday girl, leaped to her feet with an empty glass and bid Donna farewell. It suddenly occurred to us that the birthday girl had gotten little focus. A psychic should sense when the party is over; it's called reading the room. Donna put on her rope sandals and started collecting her goods: a

fringy leather purse, a nylon wrap, and an empty Star-
bucks cup. "Donna," I said as she counted her money like
a payout at the track, "I wanted to discuss maybe having
some future readings?" She smiled so hard I could see
the pale creases under her copper foundation. "Oh yeah,
come walk me to my car." Donna had a faded sky blue
Dodge Dart with an underlay of rust. She opened the
trunk and tossed her bag and the empty cup into the
mess of jumper cables, bags of kitty litter, and a box of
head shots. Yes, head shots of Donna, circa Shields and
Yarnell, sporting a razzle-dazzle smile and permed hair.
"Oh, you're an actress?"

"Oh yeah. Mostly commercial auditions now." It
didn't compute. If she had this otherworldly superior
power, wouldn't it have been used to further her thespian
career? Suddenly, my spiritual guru seemed as omnipo-
tent as the guy who makes my egg and cheese sandwich
at the deli on Sixth Avenue. But again, I was not going to
judge her on her success or even the fact that she owned
a cat.

And then there it was, in the side pocket of the fringe
purse (imagine something Cher hit Sonny with). It had
been unearthed by the collision with the kitty litter. An
illuminated iPad. A Google page on Ali Wentworth. A
flash of images of my last book cover, talk show appear-
ances, and eye surgery. My cheated heart sank. I had
been duped. Conned by the Lady Donna. She wasn't

stealing muscle relaxants from Tina's medicine cabinet; she was getting CliffsNotes on my life from social media.

My elder daughter recently celebrated her twelfth birthday. We have a tradition in our family that on your actual birthday you can have dinner at the restaurant of your choice. Nobody ever opts to stay home and have my halibut lasagna. For the past few years we have celebrated my younger girl's birthday at Benihana's (catching a flying shrimp in the paper chef's hat never gets old). But this year my almost teenager wanted something swank and chichi. She chose Nobu, a super-hip haute sushi restaurant chain with outposts in pockets of expensive real estate from Aspen to Dubai. The menu of yellowtail with jalapeño, black cod miso, and monkfish pâté is not the usual or even appropriate request from a kid, but it beats the germ-infested Chuck E. Cheese. But she opted out of a class party with all its neighbor-disturbing mayhem and crushed Oreo ice-cream cake (which lives permanently in the jute living room rug from last year). But most important—I love sushi!

Since my husband gets up at 3 A.M. every day, our typical 5:45 P.M. reservation was easily attainable at even a trendy eatery co-owned by Robert De Niro. The four of us were sitting at a round table in the middle of the floor nibbling edamame, like squirrels, when my daughters froze, mouths agape. "What? Hello? What are you looking at?" I was concerned that they were seeing a live tuna being sashimied.

"Why aren't you breathing?" I barked. My little one just pointed. I whipped around and peered into the more prestigious and desirable booth behind us, and there they were, pop-culture royalty in the flesh: THE KARDASHIANS! Before you squeal, pee your pants, and drop this book, it was not all of them. There were Kris, Kylie, and Kendall (as identified for me by my awestruck nine-year-old).

It would have been easy for me to segue from mocking the inflated prices of raw abalone and bitter mango martinis into a routine on the "famous for being famous" family of endorsement deals, perfumes, and sex tapes, but I refrained. Who was I to judge anybody? They were just a mother and her two daughters, just like us. And they were laughing and joyous (and very beautiful and dressed way better than we were). My kids were unabashed stalker freaks, and finally, as the bevy of waiters arrived with candle-lit mochi ice cream, singing "Happy Birthday," a sweet Kris Jenner and stunning Kendall Jenner approached our table. "Happy birthday! How old are you?" Kendall asked my awestruck daughter.

"Twelve!"

"Twelve," repeated Kris. "That's a great birthday!" They waved and bounced back to their table, where a small circus was swarming.

Although I will never give credence to palm readings, astrology, or tarot cards, there is one thing I know to be true: I love Kendall Jenner!

CHAPTER 5

....

That Stinks

TO BE A CHRISTIAN MEANS TO FORGIVE THE
INEXCUSABLE BECAUSE GOD HAS FORGIVEN THE
INEXCUSABLE IN YOU.

—C. S. LEWIS

I've done some inexcusable things—my brother and I once ran out on our check at the Redondo Beach Chart House, but then realized we'd valet-parked and the waitress caught us waiting for our Toyota Corolla behind eight other people. But how do I know if God exonerated me? I never received a "like" on Instagram from @TheHolySpirit. God is all about forgiveness; it's part of his brand. And I suppose if God forgives then we should all have forgiveness in our hearts, but does it have to be for everyone?

I guess we have to define inexcusable. If you accidentally smear raspberry lip gloss on an expensive ivory blouse and then don't buy it, is that inexcusable? Or just hijinks? When I was a little girl, the housekeeper was cleaning the birdcage and vacuumed up my canary. I think I forgave her; it all got overshadowed by the fact that she was dealing heroin out of our home. But I did hold a grudge. Can you forgive and still hold a grudge? According to Hebrews 10:17—when God is truly forgiving, "their sins and lawless acts I will remember no more" (direct quote from the Almighty himself). I think if someone shot me, I would struggle to forgive, even if God pulled me up by the shoulder and sat me directly across from the guilty culprit. Well, the culprit would have to be really sorry and cry really hard. And whittle a bracelet out of the pieces of shrapnel taken from my chest. And write a pop song about me. So, yes, maybe then I would forgive. Oh, wait, but if I was shot in the face like Mary Jo Buttafuoco, then forget it, I could not forgive. Did she ever forgive Amy Fisher? I can't fathom God forgiving Amy Fisher because I believe she's still doing porn.

Let's not go to extremes or I will start listing every

Fascist dictator I refuse to forgive. The matter at hand is: how do I forgive on a pedestrian daily basis? And how do I forgive as a New Yorker? Yesterday, a Japanese tourist was pushing the turnstile at Bloomingdale's with such Godzillian force it crushed my bag full of vitamin C eye cream. He never uttered an "I'm sorry" (he may not have spoken English), but not even a bow? And yet, I forgave. Quietly, to myself. As I did the meter maid who gave me a ticket for an expired inspection sticker. I placed the ticket on the Audi parked in front of me. Hopefully, they will forgive me and pay it.

There was a recent incident, however, that required Herculean levels of forgiveness. It still irks me.

I was shooting a video project in my apartment, which involved a skeleton film crew invading my home to shoot a few hours a day for about three weeks. It was not an optimal situation, but for budgetary reasons, the only way. There were a producer, an assistant, a sound guy, and a cameraman. I will call this cameraman Hugh. But don't imagine Hugh Grant; picture, if you will, Dog the Bounty Hunter.

One morning after we shot for about an hour, I was wandering down the hallway to my bedroom to fetch my reading glasses when I was blasted by a stench so overwhelming and fetid, it fogged my lenses. I assumed

one of our dogs had eaten another rotting possum car-
cass and thrown it up. I sniffed around like the evil child
snatcher in *Chitty Chitty Bang Bang* until I reached the
powder room. A room with crisp linen towels and a
vanilla-almond-scented candle, a room preserved only
for my mother and British people.

I felt a rush of fury ascend through my body. What
revolting degenerate evacuated their bowels in the only
sanctuary of true elegance? I stormed into the kitchen
and eyeballed the crew like they were hash-smuggling
hippies in the film *Midnight Express*. I leered at Hugh,
who had such a complacent smirk on his bovine face that
I instantly surmised he was the criminal. It was a viola-
tion more abhorrent than rubbing up against me in the
subway or calling me ma'am (I'm not eighty years old).
When the crew left I fumigated the apartment with a
turned bottle of Chanel No. 5, which made it smell like
an old lady pickled in white vinegar. And farts. Basically, any Hallmark store.

The next day the crew showed up again, Hugh carrying a gigantic plastic Big Gulp of Dunkin' Donuts
coffee and a tripod that scraped the side of the kitchen
with the wallpaper. The very image of the eighty-four-
ounce jug of coffee caused every toilet in the tristate area
to scream.

I quickly came up with a cagey plan to block any
further powder room explosions. I simply duct-taped

the toilet seat cover to the pedestal, a bold, neon pink *X* sealing the cover. We had a mundane morning of shooting. The crew finally exited and I contemplated the fixings of my BLT sandwich. I like to add smoked Gouda cheese and extra-thick dry-rubbed bacon. I had just cut a substantial piece of challah bread when, like the black death in Crimea in the fourteenth century, I was hit with a putrid stink. I sniffed the bacon and checked my armpits. I dropped the Gouda on the kitchen floor, much to the delight of my obese dachshunds, and ran to the powder room. The tape was still intact. Naturally, I checked the sink; I mean, who knew what that shithead (literally) was capable of? I then rushed to my own bathroom. An exclusive and restricted niche in which I sequestered all my personal hygiene implements and schlocky novellas. The room reeked like a hundred dead rats in a Dumpster in July. I had once again been violated. There would be severe consequences. And if he'd so much as stolen one of my Tuck's medicated pads? I turned to the mirror and raised my index finger like the little boy in *The Shining,* "Redrum, redrum, redrum!"

Most people would plug in a Glade solid and move on to more pressing issues such as peace talks in Benghazi or if Sandra Bullock will ever remarry. But I allowed the incident to fester, leading to repeated insomnia. It was the audacity, the disregard for my personal space, the invasion of privacy. But more important, it was just fucking disgusting!

After a bowl of Honey Nut Cheerios at 3 A.M., I decided the best course of action was to talk to Hugh. I would implore him to "deal with his shit."

Now, just imagine how awkward a conversation like this would be. He was not my husband or even a close friend. Not that I could even talk to a girlfriend about this; I can't even sit on a toilet seat that's still warm. I don't even fart! I just hold it in until it comes out in the form of a sneeze. And there's no easy way to just haphazardly bring it up—"Hey, by the way, can you maybe stop taking a dump in my house and defiling all my toilets?" But the anxiety surrounding the conversation was far outweighed by the possibility of yet another feculent incident.

Hugh and I sat on the sofa and I felt like a teenager about to launch into the "It's not you, it's me" speech. But it wasn't me and it sure as hell was him. I looked down at his Reef thong sandals and fungus-infested toenails. "Listen, I'm going to need you to use a bathroom before you come over to my house in the morning." "Why?" he blurted out. I was so taken aback, I momentarily questioned his place on the spectrum. "Well," I said, as if I was speaking to a child, "because when you use my bathroom my whole apartment smells like the subway for the rest of the day, and that's with all the windows open and candles ablaze like a Christmas Eve Catholic mass." He paused. "Well, my routine is my routine, I can't control when I free the turtles." And with that, he stood up and started changing filters on the camera.

I was dumbfounded. Should I have called the union? It had officially become a workplace complaint. I wasn't sure what category it fell under: harassment? discrimination? And then it hit me: victimization. I considered a letter to multiple corporations with potential lawsuits for health being compromised. I had read as a teenager that if you breathed in someone's gas, you were inhaling thousands of particles of fecal matter into the brain. I was no scientist, I didn't even pass middle school chemistry lab, but this must lead to harrowing brain diseases. It also gave new meaning to the phrase "shit for brains."

I resolved ultimately to deal with the situation internally. (Although I had penned some impressive letters to United Airlines, Time Warner, and Google.)

The next step was to loop in my producer, James. He was a dapper, well-dressed gay man. I filled him in on "Shitgate." And James shot me a look of such revulsion you'd think I flashed him my boobs. It was far beyond his comfort zone and he quite literally washed his hands of the whole thing. It was just Hugh and me. A fecal fight club.

Finally, after another bowel blast, the epiphany came! I knew there was a toilet down in the basement of our building because I had passed it doing laundry and storing Christmas ornaments. Did it belong to someone? There was no sign on it. It was a tiny nook with a toilet, a minuscule sink, a roll of paper towels, and a grimy bar of soap. This would be Hugh's new home, quite fittingly, in the bowels of the building. It was either that or I put down newspaper and dealt with his waste like I would a puppy's.

I excitedly presented the new plan to Hugh like I had booked Springsteen for his birthday party. "No, that's not going to work," he said.

"Um, I can get you Cottonelle?" I pleaded.

He seemed nonplussed. "It's not that, I just won't be able to hold it going down the elevator. When nature calls, she screams."

I couldn't help myself. "Are you really married? I mean, someone really married you?"

I spent the rest of the shoot in my apartment dealing with one assquake after another. My dogs were so repelled they spent those days hidden under my bed next to a lemongrass and ginger diffuser.

After the last piece of equipment had been loaded onto the service elevator, I exhumed my home with cinnamon potpourri and fans. The shit storm had finally passed.

Today, there is no trace or scent of Hugh, just the lingering fury that wafts across my consciousness from time to time. And as much as I read the Scriptures, I still found it difficult to conjure up amnesty for this impure trespasser who blew mud in my safe haven.

Over time I have learned to forgive poor Hugh. After all, God did "deliver me from the snare of the fowler and from the deadly pestilence" (Psalm 91:30). I can only hope that Hugh never uses me as a reference. I can't imagine that conversation, "Yes, he's pretty good with a steadycam, but brace yourself because when he . . ."

. . . .

CHAPTER 6

Greatest Self

YOU WERE PUT ON THIS EARTH TO ACHIEVE YOUR
GREATEST SELF, TO LIVE OUT YOUR PURPOSE, AND
DO IT COURAGEOUSLY.
—STEVE MARABOLI

You may have a point, Steve, but so much depends on how one defines her greatest self, no?
Like, does Bernie Madoff believe he has achieved
his greatest self? Sometimes I think I'm striving
to achieve my greatest self, but maybe I've hit the
ceiling—maybe my greatest self is mediocre, at best?

And that's not just an excuse to get into bed with a box of Mallomars.

My grandmother used to say, "Well, she did the best with what she was given." That seems a little less daunting to me. I wonder if I have done the best with what I was given. Let's put the physical aside (cellulite doesn't bother me and nobody believes I missed my calling as a ballerina); have I maximized all that is me? And if not, can I fit it in at this stage of the game and still get nine hours of sleep a night?

The idea of living one's life with purpose intrigues me. I've wanted to be an entertainer (middle child, divorce, overweight teen) since birth. I know, little Tommy wanted to walk on the moon and Mary wanted to be president, but I yearned for nothing more than a rickety stage, a torn curtain, and a popcorn machine. In college all my friends scrambled for majors and a purpose beyond being able to guzzle a gallon of tequila upside down on the bar. I was a drama major, without hesitation. My senior year, as everyone snorted NoDoz and went through cases of Visine writing their theses, I starred in Chekhov's *The Seagull*. I did miss out on writing a hundred-page dissertation on the history of poison ivy and its effect on socialism . . . but I received standing ovations, which, for me, was far more satisfying. But I can't say, years later, that auditioning to be the thankless mom character in mindless sitcoms is living out my true purpose.

So what is my real purpose? Ultimately, it's to populate the planet. It is my duty to beget offspring and keep the human race alive. Otherwise, animals will dominate the universe; can you imagine rats ruling Wall Street and snakes Hollywood? But that's too scientific.

There is the more spiritual purpose. How do I give back, like Lauren Bush with those FEED bags? What is my mission? Well, I'm a children's and animal rights advocate. As hard as I work to abolish puppy mills and fight for free health care for all children, however, I'm not sure that's my full purpose. I'm not a policy-wonk purist. And my husband won't let me have more than three dogs.

I do fantasize about becoming a Middle East peacemaker, but don't know the difference between Uzbekistan and Kyrgyzstan. So that's out. In truth, I believe my purpose is to entertain. Not Tony Bennett or Celine Dion type of entertaining to sell out shows in Vegas so much as a kids' birthday party artist. I'm in my wheelhouse when I can pull a rubber chicken out of my ass.

I think to even endeavor to be a performer takes a tremendous amount of courage. Nobody goes into the entertainment industry shyly and with trepidation. You have to be either stunningly gorgeous with an ego the size of Hawaii, or so damaged that you are driven by the need to please everyone. I will never be on the cover of *Sports Illustrated* unless I focus on being a darts champion for the next decade. I fall more into the category of need. But the need has to be so great that you are willing to walk into a room of studio executives in Armani suits and dance like a monkey for their approval (and, ultimately, a fairly small paycheck). When I think of the times I schlepped a bag of wigs out to some basement cattle call in the San Fernando Valley, well, I'm lucky to be alive and not featured in some out-of-focus porn film.

I believe courageousness takes various forms. In the beginning, it's merely summoning up the courage to not shake and have your knees buckle while you read copy for a Burger King commercial. And, like a muscle, you build and strengthen bravery. So one day when you're asked to audition for Warner Bros. and the entire NBC brass for a half-hour show called *Friends,* you're composed, polished, and skilled enough to ace it. Yes, we all know the outcome.

There was a big-shot producer (I'll call him Luke Levy) who my agents were desperately trying to hook me up with. I know, sounds like dating, but in Hollywood you are set up in blind-date scenarios with the hope that the outcome is a marriage of a potentially high-grossing product hopefully starring Robert Downey Jr.

I received an e-mail from Luke Levy's assistant

informing me that Mr. Levy would be in New York and would like a meeting. He asked me for a couple of times that worked. I was very honest and admitted I was completely free all week except for school pickup in the afternoons and a teeth cleaning (which I could easily cancel). I've never been deft at playing hard to get; I'm grateful at meetings when they offer me bottled water. So, we confirmed Tuesday at noon at his hotel (the Ritz-Carlton). Don't worry, this will not be a story about how I was thrown up against the wall by an over-sexed, Viagra-popping Hollywood idiot. I've never had the pleasure.

On Tuesday morning I went through my routine prep for a professional appointment: I actually shower, shave my legs, and apply foundation and concealer. Then I test-drive some outfits from my college ward-robe. And if it 1) fits and 2) isn't stained, it's the winner. I down a cup of PG Tips strong British tea to give me a bump, throw a puppy pad over the puddle of pee on the kitchen floor, and race to the elevator. A lint brush and perfume are reserved for heads of networks and foreign dignitaries.

My taxi pulled up in front of the Ritz just as I re-ceived an e-mail from Mr. Levy's assistant. "Ali, so sorry, but Mr. Levy has been pulled into a lunch and has to cancel the meeting. Can you maybe get together at some point late this afternoon?" I felt a rush of fury. He was pulled into a lunch? Really? A group of Islamic extremists threw a burlap sack over his head and dragged him to a salad buffet? We had a meeting scheduled to begin at precisely that minute!

I paid the taxi and started pacing outside the hotel. My initial thought was, well, I guess I could go and buy some more Crest whitening strips before I walk home . . . but then a stronger, more defiant voice emerged: How dare he cancel? And what was I going to do now with freshly shaved legs that smelled like coconut? Just because this lionized man had produced some edgy television with a high boob quotient didn't allow him to override a commitment with me for some overly priced Cobb salad. His time was not more precious. I refuse to believe in the hierarchy of any industry. I know plenty of wealthy and powerful people that my nine-year-old could beat at Candyland.

So with conviction (or as my dad says, pluck), I marched into the hotel. I scrutinized the woman at the concierge desk as if I had just purchased the whole chain of Ritz-Carltons and she now worked for me. Just as she was inquiring if she could assist me (or call security), it dawned on me that if Mr. Levy really was pulled into a last-minute lunch, it would be in the restaurant of the hotel. I took a deep breath (like Marlene Dietrich would inhale a Lucky Strike) and traipsed past the hostess, through the lobby, and into the belly of the formal dining room.

I had Googled Luke Levy so I knew I was patrolling for a gym rat with wispy blond hair and a year-round tan. I clocked a round table of eight men in the coveted leather banquette. There were a couple of executive types, two action stars, some entouragers, and Luke Levy. I dodged a waiter with a tray of iced Frappucinos and tapped Mr. Levy on the shoulder.

"Hi, I'm Ali Wentworth!" I exclaimed, looking down at him. Mr. Levy jumped to his feet like I had caught him measuring his own penis.

"Listen," I continued, "I just got the message from your assistant. Just now. So I thought since I was already here, I'd come and say hi and let you know that I'm slammed for the rest of the day. Maybe we meet next time in Los Angeles?" I was still peering down at his peroxided hair plugs.

Mr. Levy excused himself from the table. The posse looked at me with respect and curiosity. If I knew how, I would have gestured "peace out" as I departed.

Mr. Levy walked with me into the hotel hallway just outside the restaurant. "Listen, Ali, I am so, so sorry about this. I have a film and we're in danger of losing the lead—"

"Hey, Luke! Don't even worry about it. We're both incredibly busy people and things come up. I'll see you in L.A.!"

Every time I tried to exit he would block me with his

overly pumped bicep, begging for a few more seconds of face time.

"What is it that we can do together? Do you want to act? Are you writing?"

"All of it, Luke, all of it." I tipped my head.

"Let's come up with something that we create and you star in?"

"Maybe, Luke, maybe," I said, arms crossed. "But you're being rude to your guests. Why don't we set up a phone call to discuss?"

Mr. Levy looked back at the restaurant. "They're fine. I really want to talk to you!"

"That's great, but I'd rather not discuss projects in the hallway of a hotel."

"Will you come join us for lunch and then after—"

"No, I wish I could, but this afternoon is crazy for me." This was not a lie; I had to help my third-grader build her colonial shop for a school project. She was a tobacconist.

I walked toward the door. Mr. Levy followed and gave me a hug.

"Call me!" he said as I disappeared through the revolving door.

As I walked by the oversize windows of the hotel restaurant, I glanced at the A-list table as they watched me march with dignity down the street. Little did they know my socks didn't match!

It's irrelevant whether I did a project with Luke Levy or not. The triumph was mustering up the courage to believe in the value of my purpose and myself. For lunch I treated myself to a Philly cheesesteak hero; after all, it was a big day for me: I had grown a pair of balls.

PART II

Marriage

· ·

HERE'S ALL YOU NEED TO KNOW ABOUT MEN AND
WOMEN: WOMEN ARE CRAZY, MEN ARE STUPID.
AND THE MAIN REASON WOMEN ARE CRAZY IS
THAT MEN ARE STUPID.

—GEORGE CARLIN

· ·

CHAPTER 7

. . . .

Grounded

There's something I've never understood. You know
that famous scene in *Love Story* when Ali McGraw
tearfully looks up at Ryan O'Neal after a lovers' squabble and sniffs, "Love means never having to say you're
sorry"? How did Erich Segal get away with that? I
mean, how did his marriage work? "Listen, sweetheart,
I think you need a face-lift, I gambled all our money
and I banged your sister . . ." Then just silence? No "I'm
sorry" ever? For me, love has always meant saying sorry
repeatedly, even if it's not my fault. Sometimes I'll say
I'm sorry just because I'm too exhausted, I don't want
to fight anymore, and I know he wasn't really checking
out that jogger. Hormones. I don't think, however, that

an apology is a blanket "get out of jail free" card either. Forgiveness must be earned and forgiveness must be sincere. My daughter recently worked herself into a rageful lather because I forgot to plug in her flat iron. She called me an idiot. Granted, there may be some truth to that, but you are not allowed to call me an idiot unless you're over twenty-one. Or you are my parents. But moments later, when she realized that her nasty remark would result in her phone being confiscated for the weekend, she threw herself upon my mercy with choruses of "I'm sorry." She wasn't sorry. She was terrified she wouldn't be able to tweet duck face selfies for forty-eight hours. I call that forgiveness in sheep's clothing. (Sheep's clothing from Forever 21.)

Last Christmas I learned a valuable lesson in forgiveness. Even though inspirational quotes can nail it in a sentence or two, sometimes one needs to live the lesson to understand it. Okay, I just created an inspirational quote. I'm going to register it with the Writers Guild. Don't steal it! Look for it on Pinterest! One more time: "sometimes one needs to live the lesson to understand it."

My husband and I had planned a family vacation to Spain. Would our kids have rather gone to Atlantis or Legoland? As much as we like water slide adventures that use sixty million gallons of water, we wanted to inject a little culture in them beyond the food stand "brats and balls" (yes, sausages and meatballs). We planned a few days in Madrid and then a couple of days in Seville. We bought a Spanish-English dictionary and began counting French fries in Castilian at dinner. Even though we would be in Spain for only a week, we were pretty confident our children would come back fluent.

The night before we departed came the tedious ritual of packing. I can put a year's worth of clothes in a Ziploc bag. It's like I've been on the lam my whole life. My daughters, however, are meticulous wardrobe connoisseurs and lay each outfit on the bed as if they are attending the Met ball every night. And the amount of stuffed animals needed to accompany us? A bulky Chihuahua that lived on the bottom of the closet was suddenly taken off death row and granted carry-on status. I had to explain that the hotel would have soap and shampoo and that the gorged duffel of every hand soap, sunscreen bottle, and dishwasher detergent in the apartment would be confiscated at security. After hours of arguing over why our eight-year-old could not bring a live guinea pig and why it wasn't reasonable for our eleven-year-old to bring her pogo stick, we were packed and loaded.

We were taking the night flight (our favorite time to fly), which meant a sleeping pill for me and eight straight hours of *Gossip Girl* for my kids. They always awaken me midflight to ask what things like "hooking up" and "asshat" mean.

(Asshat, noun–Someone who has made so much

more than an ass of themselves, it's as if they're wearing their assery as a hat.

Example: "Did you hear about Joe? Jennifer turned him down and now he's talking trash about her for no reason. What an asshat.")

But they're resilient girls and don't need twelve to fourteen hours' sleep like I do. And that's when I'm not depressed.

We have a ritual before air travel of eating a delicious early dinner at home so we don't get constipated on pretzels and Bloody Mary mix. And then it was off to the airport. I carried my bag (baby pouch), my husband carried his bag, and the cart bore the heap of Hello Kitty suitcases to the gate. We were jet-setters. In our sweatpants and neck pillows. Except not on a jet. We were American Airlines miles-setters.

We handed the representative our passports and heaved the girls' luggage onto the belt. I gazed at my husband with an enamored expression as if to say, "Here we are! Our little family setting out on an adventure that will eventually become a Shutterfly album that we will force upon our friends."

The representative eyed me like I had farted on her shoes. "You're not going anywhere tonight!"

"Excuse me?" my husband politely inquired.

"The children's passports are expired," she said, throwing them down on the counter in disgust.

In the movie version, the camera would have zoomed in on my pupils, widened in sheer panic. I never checked their passports! They were kids. Their passports were as real as their American Girl ones. Oh God, it was my fault. It was my responsibility. I screwed up. My head started spinning and, like a drowning victim, I splashed around trying to grab any excuse to pull myself out of the mess. "I did, I thought . . . wait, was I supposed to . . . I never got an e-mail? They should be responsible for their own . . ." I let myself sink down into the shame of my stupidity. And then, like any mature adult, I turned and ran away.

My eight-year-old found me seated amidst an Indian family who were fastidiously plastic wrapping their trunks.

"Are you in trouble, Mommy?"

"Big time, sweetie . . . What is Daddy doing?"

"He keeps taking really deep breaths, like when he's doing yoga. The lady said she couldn't put us on a flight for at least three days 'cause they're all full. Then she asked why his wife didn't check the passports." That was sisterhood for you. I couldn't believe that the sixty-year-old woman with caked coral lipstick and the body of a Boston terrier was trying to destroy my marriage. I mean, I'm sure if I took a poll, there would be a high percentage of people who at one point in their lives forgot to check the expiration of a passport. I moved my safe place to a row of dingy black chairs by the taxi stand. My daughter kept running back and forth between my husband and me like a ball girl at Wimbledon.

"What's happening now?" I asked the tiny person who had suddenly taken over the maternal role.

"He's calling the passport office and trying to get all the bags back on the cart."

I grabbed her shoulders and stared into her eyes. "Is that vein on the side of his temple bulging?" The vein was like an anger thermometer. When a taxi driver takes the wrong route on a rainy Friday night from downtown, the vein bulges so intensely it's like he grew a finger out of the side of his head.

I wanted to roll on my back, offering my belly like our corgi mix rescue dog Charlie does when he senses danger. I would surrender, I would transform myself into the role of indentured servant. I tiptoed over to my husband and pushed the cart and its heavy load like an Egyptian slave pushing clay bricks up a pyramid. If he thought I was self-punishing, perhaps he wouldn't feel compelled to tell me what a dumbass I was.

We stood in the subzero taxi line for over an hour. I kept myself occupied by eating frozen crow. In the taxi, which had the pungent smell of McDonald's fries and sour milk, the four of us sat in stewed silence. Finally our youngest blurted out, "Are you guys getting divorced?"

There was a beat. (Too long a beat if you ask me.)

"No, of course not," my master answered.

Like all children, my daughters knew shit was going down, and escaped into their headphones. Images of life as an aging cocktail waitress and single mother flashed before my eyes.

Back at the apartment, my children knew that I was still in the doghouse. They were at once elated and befuddled that it wasn't either one of them for a change, but they also felt sorry for me. My youngest slipped me a Starburst like it was a knife snuck into prison. I didn't absorb the extent of their concern until I witnessed them brushing their teeth and flushing the toilet, unprompted.

And then came the moment of reckoning. I put on my blue monkey pajamas (I don't own silk lingerie). I was just a girl, standing in front of a boy, asking him to forgive her.

We crawled into bed. Well, not really crawled, but folded in to our own respective sides of the bed. My mind raced. Should I go with hysterical tears? Light the Diptyque candle next to the bed and burn my forearm? Do that thing in bed women never want to do but save for emergencies?

My husband pulled me toward him, wrapped his

arms around me, and kissed my cheek. I closed my eyes. "I'm so so so sorry." He kissed my cheek again. "I know you are. I love you."

And that, my friends, was true forgiveness. He didn't yell once or swear or call me a fool (well, that is my family nickname) . . . He dealt with the situation rationally and maturely. He didn't rub my face in it like an untrained puppy. He didn't punish me. And like that, it was over. And thus the lesson for both of us: "If we really want to love, we must learn to forgive."

In conclusion, we were able to get to the passport office the following morning and get new ones issued. The trip was delayed a day, but still chockful of paella, El Greco paintings, and basilicas. And I did do that thing in bed women hate to do . . . #HeDeservedIt.

....

CHAPTER 8

Tug of War

It was the middle of July and I had pneumonia. Nobody gets pneumonia in July—nobody I knew even had allergies—yet there I was, bedridden, with the shades drawn, chugging antibiotics and wheezing through an inhaler. One could argue that I am a sickly person. But it's genetic. When WASPs insist on breeding within their incestuous circle, the results are sallow, chronically tubercular, and anemic offspring (see: All British people). We all look like the antique American folk paintings of babies with bulbous eyes and pallid skin.

I was a dead ringer for the elderly gentleman in a wheelchair gasping for breath in those antismoking commercials. Adding to my misery was the fact that my elder daughter, who was one week in at sleepaway camp, was miserable. Despite the camp's cell phone ban, she had managed to con or blackmail the counselors into lending her theirs, and was calling daily, crying and begging to come home. There is nothing more wrenching than a sobbing child—not a screaming child, hate those, but when it's your own child weeping . . . I have had my fair share of driving in my pajamas at 3 A.M. in a snowstorm to fetch a child who got homesick during a sleepover.

An important thing to know about my daughter is that she's an excellent negotiator (read: manipulator). She is the Alan Dershowitz of middle school. I think she should skip high school and go straight to Harvard Law, but she has to finish puberty first. She can out-debate us on every matter except fifteenth-century theology and the history of American politics as it relates to war; my husband reigns mighty over those categories. When we first broached the subject of sleepaway camp, she expounded upon the ways in which it was too far out of her comfort zone. And by comfort zone I assumed anywhere outside her purple down comforter where she reclines Snapchatting, eating old Halloween candy, and painting her toes with glittery nail polish. We introduced the enlightened idea that the camp experience would reward her with a sense of independence. Her rebuttal was, "Why don't you give me five dollars, let me walk ten blocks in Manhattan by myself to buy some eggs. That experience will make me more independent than any sleepaway camp will." My husband and I were rendered speechless for almost an hour. She can scramble my mind; sometimes when I'm trying to dispense punishment, I end up locked in my room reading, *Are You There God, It's Me, Margaret* while she's out having sushi with some extroverted adults.

By the third hysterical phone call from a cell phone belonging to a counselor named Brandy, I tried to convince my daughter to keep a stiff upper lip, pull herself up by her bootstraps, and remember that "a hot iron, though blunt, will pierce sooner than a cold one, though sharper," among other nonsensical and clichéd Puritan sayings instilled in me from my own upbringing. I then hung up and bawled like a baby. All I wanted to do was get on a magical, winged unicorn and bring her home, but I knew it would teach her nothing about independence, self-reliance, and all that bullshit. Or maybe I just wanted to go on a magical, winged unicorn. I called the camp director and tried to get an accurate temperature reading of her misery. I reached what sounded like a 1980s cassette-operated answering machine.

A few hours later Uta called me back. Uta was the

wife of the camp director and the office administrator. Uta had a strong Eastern European accent and a monotone way of speaking that brought to mind a Russian prison guard.

"Hail-o, diz iz Uta. I'm ze kimp administrator." Long pause.

"Hi, Uta! Listen, I've been getting these heart-wrenching calls and I just want to make sure my daughter—"

"Zair are no phuns allowed hair!"

"I know, yes, she must have borrowed—"

"Who dit she say she git ze phones from?"

I feared naming names in case Uta was some leftover McCarthy spy still on the red hunt. And packing heat.

"She didn't say, listen, the point is, I'm worried. She's been crying—"

Uta cleared her throat loudly. "Evry gerl has homesickness. It's nathing."

"Could you just give me updates?"

Uta answered like she was reciting the weather, or my horoscope. "Yur daughter iz surrounded by luff." And she hung up. She probably had to spit and shine her combat boots.

It was only a two-week sleepaway camp and my daughter had just one week left, so I closed my eyes and took a huge drag from my medical inhaler. And popped another steroid.

The following week, the pneumonia worsened. A simple walk to the kitchen was fatiguing. Even watching a movie would deplete me for hours (particularly the ones starring Kristen Stewart). My younger daughter and our babysitter would be out all day surfing, picnicking on the beach, and basically frolicking with joy. What normal people are supposed to be doing in summertime. Not living in a cave of darkness, despair, and phlegm. When I would hear the front door slam, I would call for them and offer them hundreds of dollars to fetch me a Bagel Bite or some peanut butter on toast. How quickly they had forgotten the sickly old woman who lived down the dark hall.

I was living off mini bottles of Gatorade and Wheat Thins. Meanwhile, my daughter had survived the second week of sleepaway camp. I hoped she would be filled with the feeling of true selfhood and fortitude, but instead it was pure animosity and mercilessness. In the months (and, I assume, years) to come, she would regale strangers with the story of how we abandoned her in Maine without money and food and left her to survive. Yes, her experience of tennis, riding, and campfire s'mores was on a par with being lost in the desert and chewing off an arm wedged between two boulders. They should make a film about her experience.

It was very clear that I, in my enfeebled and frail

state, would not be able to pick her up on the last day of camp. The idea of driving ten hours one way was ludicrous; a simple trip to the toilet involved resting on the side of the bathtub en route. The whole ordeal took an hour. I knew my husband could retrieve her and maybe stop for ice cream and speeding tickets and have a memorable and bonding day. And he could be the sponge for all her bitching and tales of woe.

And then the world got far grimmer outside my own miserable cocoon. On July seventeenth the Malaysian airline flight MH17 was shot down. My husband was called to the anchor desk at ABC, where he sat for hours and hours of breaking news. In between throwing questions to correspondents regarding the developing investigation into a possible missile fired by Russian rebels in the Ukraine, he would e-mail me about camp. "You're going to have to go get her!"

Huh? I pulled the chilled washcloth off my fiery forehead. I e-mailed him back.

"Fever. Delirious. Can't."

Surely they would have to go back to their regularly scheduled programming; Rachael Ray was mid Naked Chef stew-off. And then he could drive up to Bangor?

The news coverage grew more gruesome. I took a fistful of Tylenol and wrote, "Why don't we get a babysitter to get her?" As soon as the network broke to a dependable health care commercial, I received his answer.

"No, after all she's been through it needs to be a parent."

This was one of those marital moments known as a power struggle. In most cases, my husband always trumps me. But on this particular occasion, I would say a winner was not so easily pronounced. Yes, he was anchoring pressing news, but I was deathly ill and literally physically incapable of the task at hand. He was the one who didn't want anyone but a parent to pick her up. And we were the only parents. There are moments when sister-wives seem compelling.

"Honey, I cannot operate a vehicle. I will drive off the side of the road. I can barely keep my eyes open e-mailing this now!" With that, I passed out.

I opened my eyes minutes later to this: "Honey, I can't leave work. What if you get your mom or someone to drive with you?" It was getting heated. Even though we both understood the other's predicament, we were standing strong. Or in my case, lying down strong.

I am always one to play the martyr card and even in my addled state recognized an opportunity to not only resent and bottle rage, but also emerge as the most magnanimous saint north of the Hudson. I would go in my soiled nightgown with a thermos of Theraflu and a box of Kleenex and save our child.

"Fine (cough cough), I'll go . . ." Slam phone down.

It's amazing how self-righteousness can spike adrenaline when driving long distances. I groaned out loud like a cow in labor. I cruised with the windows down, my chest feeling hollow, but enjoying the landscape of upstate Vermont and New Hampshire midsummer. It reminded me of my college days in vintage sundresses and bare feet skinny-dipping in lakes and eating tempeh wraps made by vegan hippies in Woodstock. And there I was, a grown woman (who would never let anyone see her naked) consuming beef jerky, driving up 95 north to deliver her daughter home. A daughter who was not jumping nude into sparkling lakes, but hiding under the infirmary cot with Brandy's stolen cell phone.

I felt old. And the pneumonia and difficulty breathing exacerbated that feeling. I reminisced about the long-haired guy with a lisp who used to recite his awful poetry to me while I wiped pumpkin butter off his beard. I wondered if he was married. And if he was married, whether it was to a man or a woman. And then I thought about all the ex-lovers and whimsical and fanciful summer days of my youth. And then I got angry with my husband again. How dare a man let his sickly wife trek to a far-off land? He must want me to die. And why do I have to do everything? I'm the only one who empties the dishwasher, throws out moldy cheese, and picks up underwear from the floor. If not for me, the show *Hoarders* would use our episode for sweeps.

Righteous anger literally fueled me to drive above

seventy miles an hour—a feverish pace inside and out. I finally reached the quaint and bucolic town in which my poor daughter was forced to drive bumper cars and chow down on homemade blueberry pancakes. And I won't go on about the rolling hills and sparkling lake.

Needless to say, when I walked into the dorm, my daughter was giggling and hugging other adorable girls in neon polo shirts. "Oh, hey, Mom!" Oh, hey, Mom? OH, HEY, MOM? After flirting with death to save her, all I'm met with is an "Oh, hey, Mom"?

I must have looked deathly; I could feel my ratty hair matted to my clammy face. I hadn't eaten in hours. All I wanted was the chicken noodle soup from Bernstein's deli on Third Avenue. "Sweetie, is there a commissary or a vending machine?"

She shook her head. "No. We had to throw out all the care packages because we had a maggot problem."

Ah, there was my cherry on top—a maggot problem. The sight of her enormous trunk and mildewed duffels made me even weaker.

My daughter informed me that she was going to watch her friends in the swim competition. I decided I would rest for a few minutes after using my inhaler and taking my antibiotics and a steroid on an empty stomach.

I climbed up to a top bunk. There were no sheets, blankets, or pillows, just a stained single mattress. A few photos of Demi Lovato were taped on the wall and the room smelled like old feet. I didn't care; I was a walking corpse. I passed out. Or died, I'm not sure which.

In my sweaty dream state I thrashed around envisioning myself packing my daughter's luggage and soiled boots into the car. And in my dream the boots were made of lead and the car had four flat tires and I was three inches tall. There were also penguins, but I'll save that for my shrink.

Suddenly, I was nudged awake. "I can't, I can't, I can't," I screamed in delirium. I opened my eyes to my husband's face. He was in a suit and tie; his skin was caked in orange TV makeup. I shot up, barely missing a concussion on the stucco ceiling.

Knowing I would be a hot mess, he had found a way to hand over the reins at work and drove above the speed limit.

My husband packed the car and bought me a McDonald's Happy Meal. It did make me happy. And the three of us drove back to New York City. I would like to pretend "singing songs and snapping our fingers," but the time was mostly spent convincing our daughter that she actually did like camp and that homesickness was just part of the sleepaway experience. And explaining what an anxiety disorder was.

CHAPTER 9

....

Couples Therapy

My husband and I have never been to couples therapy. But if we ever did, this is how I imagine it would go:

> Int. Therapist's office. Upper West Side, NY. Afternoon.

> Husband, in a finely tailored suit and navy striped tie, and Ali, in tattered jeans and looking like a bedraggled Bennington college student, sit on a tweed love seat holding hands.

Dr. Love sits across from the couple in a leather wingback chair, holding a notebook and pen.

DR. LOVE: So . . . what brings you to therapy today?

ALI: Um, everyone we know is in couples therapy and we aren't.

DR. LOVE: So you came to couples therapy because everyone you know goes?

ALI: Yes, sir, that is correct.

DR. LOVE: Ali, you don't have to call me sir, I'm a therapist, not a judge.

ALI: Yes, Doctor.

Husband pulls out his iPhone 6.

HUSBAND: Sorry, breaking news . . .

ALI: Syria?

HUSBAND: No. Drew Barrymore's in town.

DR. LOVE: Let's start by each of you telling me the one thing in your marriage you want to work on.

Husband is replying to e-mail.

ALI: I never understood why shrinks have African masks. Was therapy born in Uganda? Or is it a literal shrinking heads metaphor? Did you buy them from the guy in front of the Whitney Museum?

HUSBAND: I think we could both appreciate each other more in our marriage?

ALI: That's dumb.

DR. LOVE: That's not appreciative, Ali. There is no such thing as dumb here. It is a safe haven

ALI: Well, every couple says that. I would like to be appreciated more, sure, but if my husband followed me around telling me how wonderful I was and throwing peonies at my feet, I think it would get annoying. Appreciation is overrated. If I cook a crappy meal, I don't want to hear, "This is the most delicious cod I've ever had." I know it's bullshit! I'm eating the same dry fish, so the compliment is meaningless—in fact it's worse than that, it's humiliating. But a week later if I make the same cod dish, but with more lemon and butter and it is delicious and he says so, the compliment means more because it's true.

HUSBAND: (Looks at Dr. Love) I don't, I'm not . . . this is where it gets tricky for me!

DR. LOVE: Ali, you seem angry . . .

ALI: I'm not angry. And if I am it's because of superficial things like I'm getting older, I'm afraid of death, and I'm really out of shape.

DR. LOVE: Tell me one thing you think you could work on in your marriage.

ALI: I wouldn't mind bringing in someone new to the bedroom?

HUSBAND: *(Elated)* Really?

ALI: No. Not really.

Husband looks down.

ALI: I'd like to revise what my husband said earlier . . . I don't want him to appreciate me more . . . I want him to feel like he exceeded every expectation by getting me.

DR. LOVE: What do you mean by that?

ALI: I mean, I want him to feel like he hit the jackpot! He got a hole in one! Struck gold! When a stunning woman in tight lululemon leggings struts by, I want him to think, "Sure, she's younger and fitter and probably makes a real effort in bed, but nothing beats my wife and her winning personality!"

HUSBAND: I do, honey.

ALI: But I wish you were slightly more repulsed by all other women! And it wouldn't hurt for you to clap when I step out of the shower!

DR. LOVE: That seems a bit narcissistic.

ALI: Whoa, whoa, whoa . . . Doctor, if I read the American Board and Academy of Psychoanalysis certificate examination manual correctly, you are legally not supposed to label a patient before the third session. And I am not a narcissist, I'm the opposite: I'm an insecure psychopath.

Silence.

DR. LOVE: Let's move on.

Dr. Love is furiously scribbling notes.

ALI: What are you writing?

DR. LOVE: Just some notes.

ALI: About me? Are you writing about me?

DR. LOVE: *(Obviously yes.)* No.

ALI: Look, I'm very happy, WE'RE very happy. I just . . . sometimes I wish there was just a little drama, you know? I go out to dinner with my friends and one hates her husband, one thinks she might be gay, and the other is having an affair with her chiropractor. I have nothing! I have nothing to add except things are really good, I love my husband, and I don't fantasize about women. Boring! For once, I want to have a marital problem to bring to the table!

Husband looks at her curiously.

DR. LOVE: Do you want your husband to have an affair?

ALI: No, of course not. But I want to be able to buy the apps that track cheating spouses based on iPhone location or unscramble deleted texts! Why does everyone else get to throw dishes and scream, "that BASTARD!"

HUSBAND: I would never have an affair. I love you!

ALI: *Pointing to husband.* You see?

DR. LOVE How's your sex life?

Husband is about to speak.

ALI: Let's just say, thumbs-up!

DR. LOVE: Hmmmm . . . I don't see any glaring problems in your marriage at all. I would, however, like to spend some sessions with Ali alone.

ALI: Me? Why, did my husband win? He won, didn't he . . .

DR. LOVE: There's no winning or losing.

ALI Well, how come I have to come but not him?

DR. LOVE: You seem to need therapy.

ALI: Ugh. More? Okay, how much is it?

DR. LOVE: It's two hundred dollars a session.

Ali stands.

ALI: Are you out of your fricking mind?

DR. LOVE: I've been accused of it.

ALI: Instead of therapy sessions, I will take that two hundred dollars a week—

DR. LOVE: It would actually be six hundred— I'm suggesting three times a week.

ALI: Six hundred dollars a week and purchase a pair of jeans that fit right, meet Eddie Redmayne, and discover a fat-free Orco milkshake and believe me, I will be the happiest wife in Manhattan!

Ali walks out of the office.

HUSBAND: *(Looks up from his iPhone.)* Oh . . . are we done?

....

CHAPTER 10

The Other
Good Wife

J erry Seinfeld was on to something when he proposed the notion of a marriage ref. Unfortunately, I can't find one; although there are ads for marriage refs on craigslist, they mostly only want to treat the wives. And so instead, when I have an argument with my husband, neither of us is declared the winner and I end up calling my girlfriends and saying, "I'm right! Right?"

It's very rarely black and white. You catch him in bed with your sister—black; you catch him in bed with your brother—white. Everything else is murky gray. And in those rare moments (little jewels) when it is clear that you are the winner, it's almost impossible not to crow at your spouse, "You're my bitch now . . ."

I have had arguments with my husband that have lasted until sunrise. They become more complicated and heated than a Princeton debate. But without a silver trophy or a Fulbright scholarship. By 4 A.M., like a tortured Guantanamo prisoner, I succumb and apologize for an act I can barely remember. The need for sleep far exceeds receiving the gold for being correct in assuming the giant toenail clippings on the couch were his. And I will beg forgiveness and even relinquish sex if we can just close the shades and turn on the sound machine.

And yet, hours later when he's at the office and I'm ruminating with my tea, I still call my girlfriends and say, "I'm right! Right?"

I analyze my friends' marriages like primatologist Jane Goodall does the social interactions of chimps. How do they work? How do they communicate? Why is he always beating his chest? And I speak for both humans and monkeys when I say, everyone has a complex social system and primitive communication methods, but we all strive for long-term familial bonds. Nonetheless, it is a jungle out there.

I have one friend whose husband confessed to me that during her endless verbally venomous assaults he fantasizes about pushing her down the stairs, dousing her with whiskey, and confiding in the coroner that she was a closeted drunk. Call me crazy, but that doesn't seem the healthiest choice.

Another friend argues like a gangster in prison. She throws insults and character assassinations around like a toddler with spaghetti. It's hard to get back to being simpatico after you bellowed, "I hate everything you stand for, you fucking asshole! I could cut you!" Those words build up like plaque and eventually it all leads to decay.

My cousin Lucy is a walk-awayer. If there is any sign of marital discord, she will just roll out of the moving car. She will submerge her head in a sink full of water to escape any form of altercation. Lucy could be gorging on a three-pound lobster when her husband, Pete, decides to confront her with some issues on their sexless marriage and she will, claw still in her mouth, dart out the back door of the seafood restaurant. The problem with this tactic is that you never resolve. I call it a fugitive marriage: someone is always on the run and the other is always chasing. Plus, you never get to finish a meal.

I do think it's healthy to fight. Not *Who's Afraid of Virginia Woolf?* fight, but a heated meeting of the minds. My mother always says, "Shake it out and lay it down." If not, resentment festers and you start flirting with the kids' math tutor. But it has to be specific. A positive and conclusive face-off must stick to one topic. And when it veers into "and another thing . . ." and suddenly you're yelling about the time, fifteen years ago, when he gave you a Barnes & Noble gift card for your first anniversary, then it's just emotional, histrionic laser tag. (For the record he did give me a Barnes & Noble gift card for our first anniversary.)

I have also found that even in the rare cases when I am proven unequivocally right, the payoff is most often unsatisfying in the extreme. For example, let's say that, hypothetically, I tell my husband that our friend Fanny is having an affair with her brother-in-law. The two sneak off into the basement every Thanksgiving for a little slap and tickle.

My husband will immediately shake his head. "No, that's not true."

I will then put my hands on my hips and glare. "Um, yes it is! I know for a fact! Fanny's friend Amanda told me at lunch!"

And when he dismisses my "made-up story," naturally I have to go get proof, which is impossible unless I duct-tape a nanny cam in the heating vent of Fanny's in-laws' basement in Ronkonkoma, Long Island.

A couple of years ago, Fanny and her husband filed for divorce and the secret leaked that she had, in fact, been bumping fuzzies with her brother-in-law (who is now her husband). I don't get confetti nor does my husband hoist me on his shoulders while he sings, "For she's a jolly good truth teller, for she's a jolly good truth teller." My husband shrugs and says, "Huh. Shocking."

I think whenever I am right I should get a Twix bar and a twenty-dollar bill.

My husband and I had a recent situation wherein I was, hands down, the winner! The champion! The Roger Federer of wedlock. I need to start by explaining (fully recognizing that my husband and I will ultimately get in a squabble about why I have to delete this chapter) that my spouse is a dreadful driver. He can grill a fish, but he can't come to a full stop. He can tell you the date of every presidential inauguration, but not why it's illegal to cross the double yellow line on the freeway—we have a battered Chevy Tahoe with one headlight to prove it. And the matrimonial rub is that even though he's demonstrated the driving skills of a ninety-year-old blind man, I can't tell him what to do EVER when he's behind the wheel. If I say softly, "Watch out for the baby carriage," or "Don't hit the litter of puppies," he will stew in resentment.

Why can't men be told anything? Where is that receptive chip? Even when we all had lice, my husband refused to believe he had it too. "You have lice!" I would repeat over and over as I combed through my daughters' waist-length hair. "I do not have lice," he would retort over and over. (He had lice.)

It was a luscious summer day. We were driving (he was behind the wheel, I was white-knuckling it on the passenger side) with our kids to the beach for our daughters' first surfing lesson. The car was jam-packed with wet suits, towels, pink zinc, and excitement. My husband drove down a sandy path that turned into a dune leading right for the beach. "I don't think we should drive right onto the beach. We don't have a permit for that," I said.

My youngest shouted from the backseat, "Mommy, you go crabbing and you don't have a fishing license for that."

I shot her a look. "That's different, that's survival."

My husband, realizing the tires couldn't handle the load, started reversing back on the sandy trail. Now keep in mind, there are no signs of life, not one person, one car, or a seagull in sight. The idea, I assume, was to about-face and park on the empty street. The street had a clear vista of the bay on one side and the ocean on the other. And so my husband, with a speed that generated a sand-and-pebble storm, reversed with gusto. And . . . slam! Our heads bounced back and forth like bobble-head dolls and there was a moment of silence. I turned around to check the girls; their heads were still jiggling. Was it a gigantic boulder that fell from the sky? No, he had hit a black pickup truck loaded with surfboards. We all got out of the car. Ever the peacemaker, I ran to the truck to ensure that no one was hurt. The driver was a tan, freckled shirtless twenty-year-old who seemed somewhat shell-shocked.

"Are you okay?" I said, poking my head in his window.

"Yeah, I'm cool," he said, holding up the peace sign.

"This was completely our fault. I am so, so sorry."

"Yeah, I'm cool," he repeated, holding up the peace sign.

"Let's get all your information." He got out of the truck. "I'm Ali, by the way."

"Cool. I'm Liam."

I froze. "Are you Liam the surfing instructor?"

He looked bewildered; I couldn't tell if it was marijuana, the accident, or just his natural state. "Yeah!"

Well, that was rich. There was not a soul in sight, but my husband managed to hit and destroy the children's surfing instructor, who was about to give them their introduction to the great wave-riding sport.

My husband exchanged license numbers with Liam as I surveyed the damage. I mean, how many cars must he destroy before I give him a bicycle? Honestly, a newborn could have driven better.

My conundrum was this: how to punish him without being a bitch? It needed to be announced loudly and on the record that I was right: he is a terrible driver. But I didn't want to berate my husband in front of a man who looked like an extra from *Pretty Little Liars*.

And then it came to me.

I rushed back to the Tahoe, where my daughters were listening to mind-numbing pop music sung by Ariana Grande. I pulled off their headphones. "Can you believe your dad got into an accident?" They shared a blank look. "I mean, I don't want to point any fingers, but now you're going to be late for your surfing lesson." I could see the little wires in their brains sparking. "It's going to be REALLY embarrassing for you now that Daddy totaled his car." They threw the headphones on the floor and whipped around to investigate what had transpired. "I'm just glad it's not me going out there in that rough surf with him because I would worry that the instructor would be so mad he would take it out on me. You know, make me go too far out and stuff?" I gently stirred the pot until it boiled into a frothy frenzy. "Yeesh, those waves look big." When my husband got back in the car, the girls laid in to him like a school of piranhas on pork. And what was he going to do? Yell back at his kids? They were not being disobedient or bratty; they had a legitimate reason to be angry with him. My younger daughter refused to speak to him for a couple of hours and my elder expressed existential disappointment (a ploy her dad uses with great success on her). My husband apologized profusely. He spent the rest of the day overcompensating, folding towels, opening water bottles, and acting like a cabana boy in some 1950s beach movie.

There was no satisfaction in having my children do the dirty work. (I could never be in the Mafia.) My feeling of empowerment dissipated quickly. I knew he was a horrible driver, he knew he was a horrible driver, my kids knew, Liam knew, anyone who's driven on the Long Island Expressway knew . . . so he had an accident, big deal. Why was it imperative that I win the argument of is he or is he not the worst driver in the United States?

And then I felt embarrassed. Maybe there was no winning in the ring of marriage. Maybe the winning is in the ability to accept our shortcomings. We should treat marriage like Quaker schools and have no grades. If my husband's only fault is bad driving, then I'm surely one of the lucky ones. After all, you should see the list he has on me!

PART III

Parenting

· ·
EVERYBODY KNOWS HOW TO RAISE CHILDREN,
EXCEPT THE PEOPLE WHO HAVE THEM.

—P. J. O'ROURKE
· ·

······································

CHAPTER 11

Not Without My Daughters

L et's take the kids on an adventure trip?" my hus-band cheerfully asked, looking up from the *New York Times* travel section.

"Yes!" I said too quickly.

Would I have preferred to lie on a beach with a stack of self-help books and a club sandwich? Yes, but I suffered through so many educational family trips in my childhood that it was time to subject my own children to them. Fair is fair. My older brother still reminds me of our adolescent trip through Switzerland. I was asleep the entire time even with the deafening noise of the muffler from the Volkswagen we rented. My mother rigorously traversed dangerously braided roads of the Swiss Alps with me curled up on the floor in the back. But how can you ask a girl in the throes of puberty to absorb the trans-splendidness of the Alpine region? My focus was the growing mountains on my chest, not the snowy caps of Mont Blanc. There is a solitary Polaroid from the trip of me tucked next to a picnic basket of gooey cheese and chocolate like I was being smuggled across the border.

When it came time to pick a destination for our cultural trek, we spun the globe and chose Iceland. What a blessing to detach the kids from video games, Instagram, and *Keeping Up with the Kardashians*. Now, where the hell was Iceland?

The children's first clue that vacation wouldn't be filled with virgin piña coladas and snorkels came during the packing ceremony. I have a ritual before leaving on vacations of forcing my kids to put out everything they want to bring in a pile on the bed. I then edit (sometimes secretly throwing away a questionable crop top), and what finally makes it into the duffel is at my discretion. (Extra underwear, a cardigan, and a dress that was given to them by their grandparents. It's funny how grandparents like their grandchildren to dress like the little Parisian orphan Madeline. Especially when my daughters consider Nicki Minaj their fashion idol.)

The girls produced a pile of bikinis, tie-dyed T-shirts, headphones, and a bag of sour gummy watermelons. "You won't need any of this," I said as I dropped two down coats, some hand-knit Swedish ski hats, and hiking boots on the floor. They looked at me with expressions reserved for the death of a pet.

They overheard my husband booking the fly-fishing guide and took survival measures into their own hands by downloading as many Emma Roberts movies as their iPod touches would allow before bursting into flames.

The morning before we departed, I shoehorned some PowerBars and melatonin into our already engorged bags. I was in the middle of shooting a film and called my agent to triple-check that production knew I was out of the country for the week and there wouldn't be any schedule changes. When I was younger (sigh), every time I would leave the state of California, I would get a call about an important meeting or audition that I was resigned to missing. And ultimately went to Lisa Kudrow anyway.

And then we were off to the airport to experience the delicious meal of rubbery meat and rhubarb vomit that Icelandic Air prepared for us. But, hey, you never hear of people going to Iceland for the food!

We spent an irritating upright overnight flight to Reykjavik, the girls glued to Emma Roberts, my husband and I redirecting pent-up sexual energy into competitive Scrabble games. After we landed we sluggishly made our way to the Hertz rental warehouse and received our gleaming white Volvo. I struggled to keep my eyes open and didn't fret that my husband (have I mentioned that he's a terrible driver?) was behind the wheel in a foreign country. Although I was slightly concerned when we careened onto the highway and he asked me what side of the road the Icelanders drove on. The girls were passed out in the back under a heap of down coats. If you want to travel to a spot that is the polar (and I emphasize polar) opposite of Manhattan— Iceland is your place. Hopefully you love dried fish.

We arrived at the lodge and were upgraded to the Antarctic suite, which was a modern, black-and-white room with leather pillows and ceramic penguins. It felt like a lounge at Island Records. We curled up on the black faux fur bedspread and slept for four hours. Let me add an important side note—it never got dark in Iceland. At 10 P.M. it was as bright as lunchtime in Miami, which alters your sleep schedule in a way not even a bottle of muscle relaxants can fix. It's particularly vexing when your children refuse to go to bed until it's dark outside. It became a parody on "Who's on First" as we did rounds of "We're not going to bed until it's night!" "It is night!" "But it's not dark out!" "It doesn't get dark in Iceland." "Well, we won't go to bed until it's night." "It is night!" You get the idea. When the girls did wake up at two in the afternoon, their eyes welled up at the realization that Iceland was not a Discovery Channel TV series, but their home for the next six days. And not even Emma Roberts could save them.

"Where are we going?" my little one asked, lips trembling.

"We are going to ride some Icelandic ponies!" I answered with fake excitement.

"I don't want to ride a pony!" she pressed.

"Oh, but you've never ridden an Icelandic pony!" I don't even know what I meant by that.

We finally found the barn and makeshift ski shed nestled into a moss-covered cliff. There was a tiny, fenced-in rink with about twenty ponies that had long wispy bangs and melancholic eyes. They looked like a brooding Irish rock band. They were caked in mud and horse poop from days of rain. We couldn't find the manager or anyone in charge. A small girl with white curls wearing an unkempt nightgown and mismatched boots of different sizes pounded through some puddles and disappeared up into the house. It felt like the creepy opening of an avant-garde Danish horror film.

Finally two teenagers (ginger-haired twins) appeared from a secret door in the barn and slowly began to ready the horses. And by "ready," I mean they threw on the saddles, barely tightening the belts around the girth. My younger, sensing it was not the safest environment, clutched my hand and begged us to forgo the experience. She was confused as to why we never pushed her to ride horses in the States and yet, in a foreign country with no hospital for miles and the stench of wet cement and death surrounding us, we were forcing her. I kept repeating, "Icelandic ponies?" as if somehow that would trick her into optimism.

Unsafely perched on the ponies, we started our trail ride, surrounded by a panoramic view of hills and valleys. I imagined a row of fiery red-haired Vikings standing atop one of the hills chewing on reindeer limbs and laughing at the ridiculous tourists trudging through the muck. I rode my horse at the rear in case I needed to go all *True Grit* on the situation. My children kept turning around and giving me the "When will this end?" look. When we had done a tortoiselike loop and commenced our clippety clop back to the eerie barn, my pony started to get antsy and rebel. She—her name was Hilda—started bucking and snorting, her eyes fixated on the sloppy corral she called home. And then off she went. A full-on gallop up the hill. Small stones were flying. And behind me I heard the familiar screams of terror. When I turned I saw my family racing behind me. Clearly, my horse was the leader, the Barbara Walters of the herd. There were no seat belts, so we clutched the tufts of horse hair next to the reins and held on for dear life.

We retreated to our car and began our long drive back to the hotel. We all smelled of horse, manure, and fear. I assumed that was the last pony ride for this family. And that includes carousels.

The next morning we lapped up our grain-filled porridge in anticipation of the day ahead. The girls pleaded to rest in the room and try to FaceTime their friends in New York. They had no idea what cultural ordeal lay ahead of them.

"Are you guys excited to climb a glacier?" my husband asked. It was as if he said, "Are you guys excited to do some math homework?"

Once again, we piled into the Volvo with our down coats, hats, and tears. As a parent I put on a stoic face of wonder as we neared the ragged peaks. "This is going to be amazing," I faked. I loved the idea of it, I just wasn't sure my body was prepared for it.

Our guide was an Icelandic teenager with long hair parted on the side just above his left ear. A look my older brother pioneered in the '70s with his garage band. Frank (pronounced Frunk) was as excited about taking us up the glacier as my then hysterical little one was to being there. The tears were worse than when she had eight teeth extracted.

And then came the crescendo of indignation as my rail-thin children were handed crampons (boots with metal teeth) and ice picks. Keep in mind: the metal ice picks were the same size they were. "What are these for?" The question was delivered with a mixture of horror and disdain.

"To chip the ice," my husband rationally answered.

"For cocktail hour," I said, trying to defuse the situation. It had the opposite effect.

We hiked straight up, stumbled over chipped boulders, and gasped for breath. We finally made it to the peak of the ice-and-snow-covered glacier a couple of hours later. It was not a hike; for me, it was a battle for self-preservation. My children rallied (they had no choice), but if we'd been the von Trapp family, we'd be dead. And I would have ditched that guitar ten minutes in. Frank thought it pertinent to stop every few yards and regale us with some glacier story barely understandable through his accent. One story was about a shepherd leading his sheep through the glacier to reach the grassier knolls on the other side. One of the sheep fell in a crevice and when the shepherd tried to save him, he too fell into the hole. Just as the shepherd was about to eat the sheep, he realized that the sheep had burrowed himself in the ice and built a tunnel, which led them to freedom. The shepherd and the sheep made it to the village, and in celebration of the sheep saving the shepherd's life, the shepherd cooked the sheep for the whole village to enjoy. Needless to say, my youngest burst into a fresh bout of tears. A few hours later Frank told us another tale of a father and his baby trapped in an ice cave; the father was able to save his baby by cutting off his own nipple and allowing the blood to nourish the baby. "Zat is why allza min in Iceland haff only one nipple!" I told Frank he should write children's books.

My children couldn't peel off their crampons fast enough when we reached the lava-filled parking area. I had never seen them so infuriated. Well, maybe the one time I forgot to DVR *Teen Beach Movie*.

The doors slammed and, in silence, we started the drive back to the hotel. The kids were not interested in the crashing waterfalls or bucolic pastures of goats. They were too filled with rage. "Are you guys excited about salmon fishing tomorrow?" my husband asked at the exact wrong time. At least with hiking the glacier, there was movement. I didn't quite know how to sell standing in a frigid river in a rubber suit for hours waiting for a fish to take the lure.

And then it came. The phone call from my agent.

I could be on the space shuttle, in a cave held captive by Islamic fundamentalists, or in a fjord in Iceland and my Hollywood agent would be able to intercept any Microsoft cloud and find me.

As always he cut to the chase: "Production had to move dates, they need you on set tomorrow."

I laughed out loud. "Um, I'm in Iceland on a glacier?"

He replied without missing a beat. "Yeah, I told them that. Can you be on set tomorrow?"

I wanted to do the movie, but more important, I wanted out of Iceland. "Absolutely, I'll figure out a way." I had a fleeting vision of myself in the makeup trailer, giggling and sipping tea with Nicole Kidman while my family hunkered down to another plate of poached fish in Reykjavik.

I turned to my husband. "I have to go back. They had to flip days around because of the weather and they want me on set tomorrow."

And before my husband could even process what I had said, my girls, in unison, screamed, "Take us with you!" I had secretly relished the idea of my husband fumbling to hook flies on their poles. I, of course, would be curled up on Icelandic Air watching *Grown Ups 2*.

But no such luck. When Mommy is taken out of the equation, it causes fragmentation within the ecosystem and the resistance becomes weak.

Somewhere above Nova Scotia I looked over at my gleeful children in their faux leather airplane seats flipping through *SkyMall* magazine and taking One Direction quizzes. They turned to me and beamed. They will remember the reckless canter on the pony, struggling not to slip off a glacier, and the gamey taste of venison, but most important, they will remember that when they were teetering perilously on the brink of misery, their mother rescued them.

You can't say that about the concierge at the Hyatt in Cancun.

CHAPTER 12

· ·

Awfully Crabby

I love crabs. Not the pubic lice or pets, but crustaceans. Hunting them, and then steaming the catch in Old Bay seasoning, cracking their shells with wooden hammers and picking out the minuscule bits of meat. People underestimate the skill involved in tossing a piece of string tied to a chicken wing with precision into the ocean or bay. And even once you perfect the hurl, interpreting the subtle tugs of a hungry sea spider and pulling it from the water is a whole other degree of difficulty. It's a sport, yes, a sport of endurance. I can wade in the briny surf for six hours without food or water. Crabbing offers me an adrenaline rush I don't find in any other area of my life. A primal, Darwinist mano a mano tug-of-war with a prehistoric creature with claws—and it's not a video game! Others get their endorphins pumped by gambling, shoplifting, or opioids. For me, it's the thrill of my own personal *Deadliest Catch,* but without cameras or battling forty-foot waves in the Bering Sea. I crab from the shore, in a bathing suit, wading boots, a cooler stocked with barbecue-flavored potato chips and a couple of Snapple lemonades.

When my kids were babies, they would sit under a beach umbrella on a quilt, wearing floppy hats and gnawing on apple slices while watching Mommy yank crabs out of the brackish water and screaming in delight when I got two in one net.

One afternoon last summer I decided to up my game and relinquish the chicken and string, relying exclusively on my proficient eyes and my weapon (a large net used for skimming leaves off a swimming pool) to comb for crabs. The sun was at peak strength and the aquatic decapods were scrambling for shade within the crevasses of the jetty. My younger daughter was content sitting on the sand in her little bikini and humming Katy Perry songs to bits of barnacles and whelk shells.

I suddenly spotted a large blue crab trying to scuttle underneath a rock about three feet deep in the water. As he tucked in his claws, I methodically raised my net. My face was motionless, but my eyes aflame. I was as focused as a lurcher (an Irish dog used for poaching game) to the flash of a fox's tail. And then, as I tilted a few inches forward, I lost my balance and slipped.

My body scraped down the side of an algae-covered rock. I felt my feet hit the sandy ocean bed. I quickly inspected my arms for any collateral damage, but saw only a few scrapes on my left palm. And then I looked down. There was a bloody waterfall running down my leg. I located the source: my shin had an eight-inch gash. As I stared at the chunk of white bone sticking out like an ivory piano key, I felt nothing; therefore the leg couldn't have been mine, right? The blood gushing from my leg began to color the water. The disgusting bay water filled with Canadian goose poop and dead quahogs. It's amazing how sluggishly the mind works when it's not willing to confront its own horrors. It took me thirty drowsy seconds for my leg to inform my brain that I was injured, that there was a piece of my bone floating in the bay, and that I probably needed medical assistance. It's the same passive reaction I imagine people whose limbs have been bitten off by sharks experience. You're numb and in shock and hope that you're watching a PBS documentary about somebody else's drama. And if you wait a few more delirious moments, you'll realize it was a hallucination, your leg is fine or your arm is still there, it was just a big black shadow in the water.

I looked over at my daughter who was belting out "California Girls," strutting on her seaweed stage. I felt light-headed. Thank the good lord our babysitter, Cherie, had just shown up with sandwiches. I say that because I'd probably still be in the bay now, a corpse in tattered J.Crew shorts flapping in the wind like a skeleton in the Pirates of the Caribbean ride (the irony being that I'd be covered in crabs). "Cherie! Cherie!" I screamed. She was used to equating my excitement with shoe sales and the one time I fixed the garbage disposal.

"You get a big one?" she yelled back.

I simply raised my gory limb, which led her to dive into the surf. Cherie hoisted me to the shore like a superhero; I'll never know how, she is half my size. I could hear her heaving breaths and closed my eyes against the harsh sunlight. And then everything went fuzzy and I blacked out. When I awoke, my daughter was crying and shaking, and some women from a nearby house were tying a tourniquet of checkered napkins around my leg. They raised me up like a casualty of battle and carried me to our Tahoe, which was parked nearby.

In the backseat, my daughter held my hand. And then a strong maternal rush overcame me and I focused on the emotional toll this episode would have on her and not the throbbing pain of my largest appendage. "It's nothing but a scratch, sweetie!" I lied. "It's nothing, I'm going to be fine. What movie should we see tonight?"

She looked at me as if to say, "You think I'm an idiot?

Don't try to distract me; you think I want a one-legged mother?"

When we arrived at the emergency room, I was pushed, at a snail's pace, into the building in a wheelchair. I had envisioned people flying to get out of the way as fourteen doctors and nurses ran on either side of a gurney, holding my hand and screaming, "Stat." The staff being played by the cast of the nineties hit *ER*. But no, I was passed off at the administration desk to a woman who looked like Julianna Margulies if Julianna Margulies ate only pies and drank only lager. "Insurance card," was all she said as she mechanically extended her hand. There was no, "I see that you're covered in blood, in a great amount of pain, and about to vomit . . . how can we help?"

I filled out a clipboard of forms. Did I have to enter the hospital carrying my own leg to rouse any concern? At that point I was so delirious, I think I may have charged my hospital stay to an old boyfriend.

I was told to wait. Okay, fine. I sat in the sterile waiting room with *Better Homes and Gardens* magazines from 2001, blood-soaked napkins knotted around my leg, and a hysterical eight-year-old. Good plan. At one point a very bored woman (whose daughter had a sprained ankle and was getting X-rays) turned to me and said, "I think you're so funny! What are you working on now?" On what planet, looking at the state I was in, was that question appropriate? Of course, I not only answered her but also launched into my top-ten favorite movies and why, in my opinion, Sly Stallone's comedic chops are always overlooked.

A nurse came over—with a painkiller, I prayed—and asked if someone could please remove my daughter. I suppose a shrieking little girl in a blood-spattered bikini was unsettling for people doing crossword puzzles and sipping cold coffee. Cherie covered her in an old sweatshirt and drove her home.

I was taken into the heart of the ER with its stretch of beds divided only by sheets. As I lay on my cot, I counted the pockmarks on the stucco ceiling and listened to the groaning woman next to me. I shuddered to think what her diagnosis was. All I knew was that it involved salad tongs.

And like a game show host, the sheet was whisked open and a young doctor appeared. "Hi! I'm Dr. Cole!" Dr. Cole looked like one of my kids' camp counselors. His hair was a little long and unkempt and he was too tan to be an ER doc. He inspected my slash and swiftly responded, "Okay, well, I'm going to inject a Novocain-type substance into the wound and after about thirty minutes stitch it up!"

I sat straight up. "You're going to stick a needle in my leg?"

He nodded.

I blacked out again.

An hour later, once again, the sheet was wrenched open in a swift and terrifying manner. My friend Holly, who lived nearby, had come to the hospital to check on the severity of things after I texted her a photo of my wound. "Jesus Christ!" she shrieked when she saw it in the flesh (yes, pun intended).

I reiterated the plan as relayed to me by Dr. Dude. "No!" she said emphatically. "You need a plastic surgeon."

I smiled. "Oh, I don't care what the scar looks like. I just want them to sew it up so I can get out of here!"

Holly threw down her tangerine Hermès bag. "You're not going anywhere until we've seen a plastic surgeon!"

I was relieved to have someone take charge. At that point, if someone had suggested euthanasia, I would have agreed.

The plastic surgeon was a hearty man who had just pulled an all-nighter stitching up a chain saw accident. He took one glance at my leg and gasped. "Damn, this ain't no sew-it-up job. I'm putting you under general anesthesia, power washing the wound, and then stapling it up." I didn't care to know what power washing was, but the words "general anesthesia" made me so elated. Put me under, knock me out, and so long, suckers!

The plastic surgeon told me later that as they wheeled

me into the OR I looked up at him in my purple haze and shower cap and said, "Since I'm already going to be under, how about you do the boobs too?"

I woke up with a calm and harmonious outlook. My leg was bandaged up and my IV was still dripping with joy juice. It was all over. Holly was tapping away on her BlackBerry and talking on her earphone about the size of pizza ovens. I realized I loved general anesthesia. And wondered why I'm not put under for more things, like parents' night at middle school or anything that involves camping outdoors.

I was also relieved to see that my leg was still attached to my torso. I think I had a twilight night-terror that I had gangrene and Alan Alda had to amputate it.

I don't recall the logistics, but I ended up in the guest room at Holly's house. My leg was propped up on pillows and a slew of prescription vials were spilling over the bedside table. The curtains were drawn. It was quiet but for the distant giggles of children jumping in the pool. I hoped my daughter had washed the blood and visuals out of her memory. Judging from the trash can full of string cheese and candy wrappers, she seemed to be healing fast.

She later checked on me, her hand over her eyes on the off chance the laceration was still open. "I'm fine, sweetie," I purred. "See? It's all bandaged up!" She kept her distance in case it was contagious. Just before her long wispy braids disappeared out the door, she whispered, "Well, Mommy, you probably got a chapter for your book out of this!"

"If nothing else, a low-budget horror film, sweetie."

As I lay back on my pillow, relieved my child would not be scarred from the aquatic ordeal, I realized an unexpected perk: I had been treated to a mini vacation. Suddenly, there were people gathering around to make me sandwiches and entertain my girls. I no longer had to drive kids to camp, recycle cans, or even return phone calls. Now, I'm not promoting a self-inflicted injury and trip to the ER, but how many of you can say that you got to watch all five seasons of *Breaking Bad*, uninterrupted, on Percocet?

Exactly.

. . . .

CHAPTER 13

Happily Ali After

My childhood was spent taking National Gallery
tours, day trips to Monticello, and summers at
the re-created seventeenth-century farming village in
Plymouth Harbor. We never took a family trip to Disneyland, Disney World, Busch Gardens, or any of the
massive complexes that offer sausages the size of Buicks
and rides with names like the Terminator and Tower
of Terror. I missed integral childhood experiences like
watching my vomit fly backward on a ride that swoops
in upside-down loops. That said, I do know how to
churn butter and am a skilled farrier (a person specializ-
ing in the preparation and fitting of a metal horseshoe).
I was too busy climbing Mayan temples in 100-degree

heat while my friends snapped photos at faux safari game parks, sucking on cherry snow cones. And, as with most things, when you're deprived of them as a child, you yearn for them even more as an adult. My personal list of forbidden fruit includes Disneyland, TV, and prom (I went to an all-girls school). Secretly I hope that every time we go to a bar mitzvah my husband will hand me a corsage.

Then I became a mother. Maybe it was the food I consumed while I was pregnant, but my daughters were born with Princess Barbie blood. They would scamper through the aisles of Target in a frenzy, clutching all the princess paraphernalia they could carry to the oversize red cart. All I wanted was several hundred gallons of laundry detergent and a few bras. I would explain to them that by next week the Ariel doll's head would be another casualty to a mysterious toilet accident, and that we already had four Cinderella dresses. They didn't care; they wanted to consume every Jasmine multivitamin; pair of plastic Sleeping Beauty slippers; and 100 percent polyester, highly flammable Belle nightgown they could get their sticky little hands on. I completely indulged it because I didn't want to raise them Amish and the closest I ever got to dressing up as a Disney princess was when my grandma sewed me a Little Bo Peep costume for Halloween. I looked like a German beer wench during Oktoberfest. I even let my younger daughter wear a Tinkerbell nightshirt to school so often the material finally disintegrated into a ball of neon green lint.

When my elder daughter was turning six, I had the ingenious idea of throwing a *Little Mermaid* birthday party. Having patted myself on the back all the way to the mall party store, I was shocked upon my arrival to discover an entire room dedicated to Ariel gizmos. I was dumbfounded to learn that other people had thought of a *Little Mermaid* party before me! (I was a naive mom, I also believed I invented breastfeeding.) I was obsessed with my under-the-sea-themed celebration; in my dreams I fantasized about blue and teal streamers and gummy fish and dried starfish glue-gunned to the wall. My daughter pleaded for a sheet cake from Costco, but I prefer butter cream made from butter and not lard. No offense, Costco, you know you are my go-to for chicken nuggets and Q-tips. And catch me on a particularly hormonal day and I'll be facedown in a Costco mango cheesecake.

I constructed an enormous three-tiered cake from scratch, and by scratch I mean six boxes of Duncan Hines yellow cake mix. It was a masterpiece of white-and-turquoise wavy frosting, green licorice seaweed, and red Swedish fish and Haribo sour octopi. It should have been preserved in the Smithsonian instead of ravaged by a pack of six-year-olds.

I was hell-bent on throwing a blowout that the kids would remember well, at least until they were seven. I had witnessed a magician a few weeks earlier at another kid's birthday party. The illusionist didn't wear a tuxedo or a black top hat, just jeans and a Jim Morrison T-shirt. I had never met a cocky magician before. He told me Liev Schreiber was considering playing him in a movie about his life. Yeah, me too, buddy, Julianne Moore is chomping at the bit for her start date on the Ali Wentworth biopic. Chaos ensued when the magician made the mommy of the birthday boy disappear, which resulted in uncontrollable panic and a real-life rendition of *Lord of the Flies*. I found the mommy hiding in the coat closet and forced her to dump her glass of Diet Coke and bourbon and prove to the children she was alive and safe.

I considered dressing up as a mermaid. Look, I'm no Daryl Hannah, but I had a few old bikini tops, and how arduous would it be to sew on a shimmery fishtail to a pair of maternity jeans (yes, I wore them for a while after giving birth)? But kids always cringe when parents dress up; do you know how many of my mom friends are "sexy cats" every Halloween? A headband with ears and black lace lingerie is not a costume unless you're really turning tricks for treats. I perused all two of the celebrity look-alike party companies in Washington, D.C. It wasn't Hollywood, so the choices were

a little rough. I'll put it to you this way: the Marilyn
Monroe was Algerian. I finally settled on a Dora the
Explorer, real name Sandra Schlemmer, who claimed
she had some mermaid gear.

Sandra was forty-five minutes late to the party. I had
already repurposed the piñata with duct tape twice to
occupy the little darlings, who were anticipating the
surprise guest. She arrived in a fluorescent orange
wig, which was slightly askew, exposing a chunk of
ratty auburn hair on one side. She had on no makeup
and carried her tail (a tail that had seen a lot of storms
and shipwrecks). As she changed in my bedroom, I
continued escorting Sleeping Beauties, who weren't
completely potty trained, to the bathroom and help-
ing a little boy with a bloody nose from the way too
bouncy inflatable castle.

When Sandra finally entered the garden, she was
barefoot with chipped black nail polish, and a tat-
too of a skull with a snake coming out of its mouth
was clearly visible on her lower back. I handed her
some water; I figured that being half fish, she'd be
parched. And then I became Maria from *Sesame Street,*
clapping my hands and in a singsongy voice calling,
"Can all the children please gather round!" They
plopped on the grass holding melted string cheese

and with fruit-punch-stained mouths and waited. We all waited. Sandra just kept saying hi and cocking her head from side to side repeatedly. Why wasn't she singing? Twirling her hair with a fork? Didn't she have a little puppet friend who was a mackerel? Sandra did answer questions like where she went to college and if she was a boy or a girl. And then I did something more typically associated with a menopausal meltdown or an antidepressant cocktail gone wrong: I ran upstairs and started to cry. And not because I was concerned that the mermaid did not meet my daughter's expectations, but that she didn't meet mine! I wanted Ariel to come to my birthday party. I wanted Ariel to sing while animated crabs in a mariachi band played around her head.

My daughter didn't care. Kids are more simplistic than we and the whole consumer world; give them credit for that. The children at the party would have been happy running around in circles looking for a hidden stick. But I had projected this stunted fantasy from my own childhood. I had believed it was satisfied years earlier at our wedding, which also featured an ocean-themed cake with blue frosting (just without the gummy octopi). But I guess it had not.

Before Sandra left, I gave her a huge tip, a ziplock bag of leftovers, and hugged her in a way that said, "Dear God, girl, get some help!"

A couple of years later, we took our daughters to Orlando during spring break to see killer whales do flips, eat nachos at the NASCAR café, and meet a real-live princess. Really, a gift for all of us. And when we told them we were having lunch in Cinderella's castle? They screamed so ecstatically the younger one projectile-vomited all over the minivan.

It was 100 degrees in the shade and the all-you-can-eat castle special was meat loaf and gravy. Our busboy was dressed as Prince Charming (his name tag read DIRK) and he was about as charming as ringworm. His only communication was not about an invitation to the ball, but "We ain't got no Sprite, machine's broke." Still, I felt it was important my daughters knew that they didn't need to rely on a guy to liberate them from an evil spell and that even Prince Charming gets acne.

We made our way through the sea of fanny packs and denim culottes to the Snow White ride. All of us climbed into a wooden boat that was electronically towed through a dark tunnel that smelled like a mildewed basement. There were the adorable mechanical dwarves hi ho hi hoing off to work carrying mallets and pickaxes, but when we turned a corner things became less than fairy tale. Suddenly, a papier-mâché wicked queen holding an apple bolted out of the wall. My children shrieked. Yes, everyone screams at that moment of the ride, but my daughters reacted the way they do when the nurse informs them that she has to take blood. "Get me out of here! Mommy, GET ME OUT OF HERE!" My younger daughter stood up and started rocking the boat until we nearly capsized. I grabbed her and held her tightly on my lap using both arms and legs, trying to distract her by pointing out the more soothing elements of the ride, like the wooden owls and stuffed fawns with red eyes. Her screams echoed so loud, I'm sure they could hear it over at the Alice in Wonderland spinning cups. I succumbed to the fact that we would quite literally have to ride it out.

And then we saw the proverbial light at the end of the tunnel. The boat hadn't come to a complete stop before my children leaped into the arms of the Disney guides. Mind you, not our guides, just the closest people to safety. Maybe we should have taken the Sleeping Beauty ride—I assume you just climb onto a Posturepedic bed and nap? Perhaps in my infantile haste I jumped the gun a little by taking my kids when they were too young. Although my elder daughter does remember the squirrel we met in the parking lot with gum stuck to his ear.

Five years later, my dream came true again! We took another trip to Disney World! My kids were older and my legs were in better shape. I had my picture taken

with all the princesses at the character breakfast, rode
Splash Mountain three times, scored high on the Buzz
Lightyear ride, and kept my eyes open the whole time
in the Haunted House. I have to admit, Space Moun-
tain made me nauseated and my upper arms tingled, but
Avalanche was awesome and you can never do the Peter
Pan ride enough times. I purchased some adult Mulan
slippers, a giant Mickey Mouse head made out of Rice
Krispie treats, and the whole set of *Frozen* dinnerware.
Oh, my kids? They were off playing golf

. . . .

CHAPTER 14

For You, My Pet

The only thing my younger daughter wanted when she turned seven was a guinea pig. We offered bejeweled Uggs, an iPod, even the financial backing for her mayoral campaign in New York. Anything but a guinea pig. It seemed unfair that we would pay for a bi-level habitat (with organic vegetables and dried-apple hanging toys) for a rodent whose relatives I exterminate monthly by calling Bob's Pest Control. If I see a rat on the tracks of the uptown 6, I scream like Jack Nicholson just whacked an ax through my door. But a rodent I should name Bubbles, dress in American Girl doll clothes, and cuddle with?

My daughter was determined.

"We have two boisterous dogs who thrive on scent and the massacre of small creatures," I pleaded.

She wasn't swayed. "I'll keep it in my room."

We hit her with questions, like a press conference after a political scandal.

"Who is going to feed him?"

Without even looking up: "I am. Of course."

"What happens when we go on vacation?"

She sighed. "My friend Darius has his grandma take his guinea pig, Twerk, when he goes away."

I could not imagine FedExing our furry family member to my mother in Florida whenever we left town, mostly because I know she would refuse to sign for it. But more important, she'd squash it with the phone book.

When my little girl was even younger, she begged for a chinchilla. She excitedly called my husband to tell him she'd decided on her dream pet and, instead, got an intern, a twenty-year-old who thought breaking news was Britney Spears's fragrance launch. "I want a chinchilla" (said with a slight toddler lisp), my daughter announced.

"Oh, that's so great!" said the intern, who was simultaneously perusing a fashion blog. "But you don't want just one, it takes like two hundred for a coat."

My daughter is now a vegan.

We finally relented on the guinea pig, but not because we caved on the idea of fulfilling our child's dream of caring for another living creature and all the responsibility that goes with it—no, we finally said yes because her birthday was fast approaching and we couldn't come up with a better gift idea.

So she was given a guinea pig. She could choose amongst the millions of adoptable, rescue guinea hogs in the tristate area. She read the pet adoption section of the *New York Post,* spread the word at school, and searched pet rescue sites for hours. One afternoon, while I was reaching for my stash of chocolate chip cookies in the closet, I heard a shriek of "Mommy" that was more urgent than the usual "I need socks." She had found the guinea pig she wanted. Her. Him. Well, THEM. My daughter couldn't fall for a tiny little white snowball of a pet; no, she settled on two obese guinea pigs named Archie and Lenny.

"Those are two guinea pigs. We said one!" I pointed out, hands on my hips like a real parent.

"Mommy, they can't be separated. They are life partners."

Suddenly my politics were being challenged. She looked at me with her beatific face and ethereal eyes and the next thing I knew I was talking to American Airlines about flying Archie and Lenny from Pittsburgh to New York. Coach.

Pets are part of childhood. Their lives and deaths define the emotional beings of those adults the pet-owning children will grow up to be. Marilyn Monroe once said, "Dogs never bite me, just humans." As a mother, I remember all the *Marley and Me* episodes in my own life and want them for my children.

I grew up with myriad pets. Except snakes. We lived in D.C. and knew too many human ones. My older sister, Sissy, managed white mice because my mother wanted something small and contained. At the time, Sissy was reading *Stuart Little* and assumed her precious *Cavia porcellus* would wear Scottish bonnets and drive miniature red sports cars. The two beady-, red-eyed vermin lived in a small plastic container where they relentlessly scratched at the lid, exposing their pink bellies and utter desperation. They were eventually moved to her trash can because they kept procreating at a rapid pace. Female mice can have up to ten litters (about six in each litter) a year, so do that math! The trash cans got bigger as generations of white mice were birthed before our eyes. One day after school we returned to a toppled trash can. We searched for them for hours, and were haunted by their high-pitched squeaking at night. But they were never seen again. I'm pretty sure we moved not because my parents wanted to downsize, but because they were overwhelmed by the infestation and it was the only alternative.

My brother John was partial to the basset hound. When he was twelve he was allowed to choose any breed of dog he wanted and the symbol of Hush Puppy, the premier footwear of the decade, was the winner. Aside from the dwarfism, ear mites, spine injuries, and yeast infections, Josephine was the perfect dog. We could hang from her pendant ears without incident and her forlorn eyes always ensured much petting and attention. Josephine was slovenly; her belly brushed across the marble floor when she walked from room to room. And her barking resembled the sound track to any 1970s prison-break film. When Josephine was a couple of years old, she took a dark turn toward canine juvenile delinquency. She decided that Kibbles 'n Bits was not going to cut it anymore and began hanging outside our local Safeway for a bigger score. Josie would enter the store like any housewife doing errands, bypass produce and the sale on instant soup, and make a beeline for the meat department. There, she would sniff out a choice cut of New York strip steak (or, occasionally, a pork loin), bite down, and carry the package back out the door and into the parking lot, where she would consume it delicately and unrushed. She was known as the smash-and-grab pooch. And if that were not enough, after her feast she would be so bloated and fatigued that she would stagger onto Massachusetts Avenue, one of the busiest and most congested streets in D.C., and curl up for an afternoon snooze. Traffic would halt, people would exit their cars blustering, and if anyone tried to move her by pulling her tail or gently kicking her belly, she would growl and send the terrorized person back into their Acura. These jaunts became as frequent as the D.C. police's arrest threats. Sadly, the day came when Josephine was forced by the city of Washington, D.C., to move outside the district borders. We were told she was moved to a free-range felon farm. Mutts behind Bars. Somewhere sweet Josie is some dingo's bitch.

When I was twelve and my older siblings were sent to boarding school (another free-range felon farm), it was finally my turn to choose a pet. I took the task very seriously and methodically scoured the public library for pet encyclopedias and almanacs that I would drag many blocks home. My kids don't know how lucky they are to have Google. I would lie in my bed with a flashlight and try to imagine myself with an Irish setter, a French bulldog, or a spider monkey. I finally chose a dachshund. And have been an avid dackel lover ever since. I share this adoration with other famous dachshund owners— John F. Kennedy, Picasso, Andy Warhol, Jack Ruby, Abraham Lincoln, the Olsen twins, and David Hasselhoff. But don't hold that against the breed.

For many young girls their first love is a horse, but mine was a little black-and-brown sausage named Max. Freud would say a penis substitute; Woody Allen would say, "For you I'd think a Great Dane!" I slept on the floor next to Max's dog bed before he was housebroken, dressed him in my old Cabbage Patch doll clothes, and shared mac and cheese with him out of the same bowl. Aside from my husband, Max was my only kindred spirit and confidante. Until Chester, Gilbert, Charlie, and Daisy. And all the dachshunds that followed him.

I didn't mean to rescue Gilbert. I was at the East Los Angeles pound searching for a friend's lost dog and there he was. Gilbert was skeletal, wrapped in one of those quilted blankets used for moving, and shaking uncontrollably. One of the volunteers held him as he trembled, peering out from behind the cloth with Norma Desmond eyes. I never walk away from an adoptable dachshund. Or any form of gingerbread. Those are just my rules. So Gilbert joined me in the Hollywood Hills. Like any new relationship, it took some time for us to ease into cohabitation. I found that, like a few men I had dated, Gilbert had the nasty habit of peeing around the sofas and chairs in some kind of alpha ownership ritual. Something I could never train him, or any other dachshund, out of. But eventually we existed in a harmonious, symbiotic union. The phone would ring and he would yap incessantly. The phone would ring in a movie I was watching and he would yap incessantly.

Gilbert was a burrower and slept under my down comforter deep in the bowels of my bed, where he would curl himself up like a Cinnabon until morning. My own cashmere water bottle. Until he started licking his own ass; then he was back to the dog bed.

We had owned a small cottage in East Hampton, Long Island, for many years as a refuge from the humidity and tempers of Manhattan. Gilbert would bark at the surf like its monstrous hands were flowing up to seize him and swallow him back into the sea. And he would chase deer because somewhere in his tiny DNA he believed he was bred to slaughter lions. I don't think he thought through how he would transfer his carnage home; he struggles to lift a sparerib.

We sold that house and years later rented a house in Amagansett, which was about twenty miles east. It was more desolate and quieter and what I imagined the Hamptons were like in the 1950s. I would have eaten melon topless with Pollock and sketched the dunes with de Kooning whilst Coltrane played his sax and Kerouac rolled joints. But it was the twenty-first century, so I drove my kids to craft camp, argued with the neighbor about spilled garbage, and ate gluten-free blueberry muffins. My husband ceremoniously took Gilbert for a daily constitutional on the beach. One afternoon it was near dusk and overcast. As the front door opened, I faintly heard, "I lost Gilbert!"

"How could you LOSE Gilbert?" I said, panicked.

"I think I saw him walk into the surf," was his imbecilic answer.

Dogs are not suicidal and Gilbert was not some despondent Geraldine Page character who lost the will to live and walked dramatically into the waves. He was lost. Or found a better family with panoramic views and a tennis court. I painted signs and stapled them to every tree and post in a mile radius. I called animal control and the mayor. The mayor never returned my call. And for three days and two nights we waited for a sign, a whimper, a tepid scratch at the door. I couldn't sleep, imagining Gilbert, face to the storm, struggling to brave the elements.

On day three, we got a call from animal control. They had found a dachshund in the town of East Hampton. To be more specific, on the roof of the town hall in East Hampton. My husband reluctantly drove over, knowing that, given his age and minuscule legs, our ten-year-old, white-whiskered banger couldn't have trekked twenty-three miles.

We were wrong. Gilbert had lost half his body weight and was covered in burrs. Yes, he was lost, but being the determined little German that he was, he had marched miles to the only turf he knew, a place where we had lived for many summers before. We will never know how he ended up on the roof of the town hall, but then, who built Stonehenge and where is Jimmy Hoffa buried?

And so the next generation of pet fostering commenced. Archie and Lenny, the aforementioned guinea pigs, arrived at JFK Airport in a crate that had a small sticker slapped on one side that read FRAGILE. In honor of the two furry newcomers, I baked two red velvet cakes in the shape of guinea pigs and frosted them in their specific brown and white colors. And then we hacked into them with a knife and ate their innards.

Archie and Lenny took over our daughters' bathroom like an episode of "Hoarders: Rodents" where their poop (which looked like brown Good & Plenty candies) dusted the white ceramic tiles. They ate better than the majority of Americans and smelled like an indoor, heated petting zoo. But they were our pets! And as much as my husband wanted to flush them down the toilet or "set them free" (guinea pigs are the only manmade animal that doesn't exist in the wild), we chose them to finish our circle of family. They completed us!

And someday Archie and Lenny will escape from their cage and find freedom through our radiator vent or procreate (Lenny might be female, we don't know), giving birth to hundreds of guinea pigs who will take over the Upper West Side of Manhattan. But no matter what the final outcome (and I'm talking to our babysitter when I say it won't be a dish involving barbecued peanut sauce), our daughter will delight in their company. And one day, she will have a daughter who will beg her for a pygmy goat or a hedgehog. And as much as my daughter won't want to clean the newspaper from beneath the bearded dragon or feed live mice to the albino boa constrictor, she will remember her relationship with Archie and Lenny and she too will indulge her daughter's request.*

· · · · · · · · · · · ·

*At the time of publication, Archie and Lenny were living with a daughter of a friend of a cousin of the priest of the Greek Orthodox cathedral in Long Island. Their names were changed to Taylor Swift and Harry Styles.

CHAPTER 15

....

Help!

Halfway through the film *The Help*, I was so hysterical my husband had to carry me out of the theater like I was having some sort of seizure. I could hear him whisper, "Bad shrimp," to the ushers. We were having a date night (or because of my husband's schedule, we call it date afternoon) and decided to see a movie. I was expecting much more of a romp. And there *was* a knee-slapping moment; poop in a pie always delivers. I mean, who hasn't done that? But it was the "You is good, you is smart, you is important" line that sent me into sniveling convulsions and prompted our early exit. After a few hours of clinging to my husband's neck and finishing my box of Milk Duds, I tried to surmise why.

The quote addresses the three integral parts of being someone worthwhile: someone good, someone smart, and someone important. (Note to my daughters: there is no "you is hot.") The fact that it's grammatically incorrect underscores the poignancy, as it is spoken in the film by a black maid in the 1960s who is trying to impart wisdom and warmth to a little girl she has cared for who never received love from her own mother. The maid expresses the only love provided in the child's life.

The quote has struck such a chord with many people, not just me, because it triggers that want and need in all of us. And by making it a mantra and repeating it on a loop, some will eventually believe it. Of course, if you're the chairman of JP Morgan or Heidi Klum, you won't need to do this.

But why does it touch me so intensely? Maybe we all yearn to hear those lines whispered to us. Am I the little girl? Or more important, am I the little girl STILL?

I was the youngest of three children and then the middle child of half siblings. I've had a mother and two stepmothers, a father and two stepfathers. So yes, the fact that I became an actress is self-explanatory if not glaringly predictable. I need love, validation, and global attention. I don't fault my parents, but our childhood does inform who we will be (no matter how much therapy we have). Honey Boo Boo anyone?

Perhaps if someone had repeatedly assured me, "You

is good, you is smart, you is important," my life would be different. I might not be on Zoloft. Or binge-eat Skinny Cow caramel and pretzel ice-cream bars at 3 A.M. What if I really believed from early on that I was good, smart, and important? I'm not saying I'd be a Supreme Court justice, but I might have tried harder to pass algebra (I only did because my teacher was arrested for sexual misconduct, so I got a pass). You is important means you have worth, weight, character, and merit. It means you matter. Tell that to Michael, the sophomore at Harvard who ditched me behind the Widener Library in 1983 holding my bra and his half-empty Heineken.

I've always been more at ease telling jokes than commanding attention for my sage opinions on North Korea's intercontinental ballistic missiles and how they've broken the armistice agreement. Even today, I find public speaking to be a herculean task; it would probably be easier for me to strip. (Nobody wants me to; believe me, I've asked.) The feeling of being important just never resonated with me. I confess, I was the kid who leaped around the living room shirtless with a pillow shoved down a pair of black tights while I pretended to be Baryshnikov. I still wear costumes on Halloween. Of course I pretend it's at the insistence of my kids. I once dressed up as Sunny von Bulow with a blond wig and pajamas stuffed with pills. My children were four and six years old. They thought I was just dressed up as me. I'm not sure if these are examples of a person who feels she is good, smart, and important.

Had Idi Amin and Pol Pot received nurturing whispers like "you is good" as toddlers, might hundreds of lives have been saved? Pol Pot was the eighth of nine kids and failed all his exams in 1953. This is not someone who felt good, smart, or important. At least the little blonde in *The Help* had a fighting chance, thanks to Aibileen. If not for her, she might have become Squeaky Fromme. I'm not saying that if every psychopath or homicidal maniac was the beneficiary of good mother messages they would all be saints; Jeffrey Dahmer would have still chewed Aibileen's arm off, but a few of the Fascist dictators might have been dulcified.

I would love to write a sequel about Aibileen and the little blond girl in the form of an action film starring Whoopi Goldberg and Dakota Fanning. The little blond girl grows up corrupt and unloved and, as a teenager, gets into trouble with the mob, drug dealers, and the Kardashians. Consequently, she is being hunted, with a large bounty on her head. At this point, Aibileen has retired (after forty years of servitude, the family gives her a monogrammed tote bag) and moves to a remote island off the coast of Trinidad and Tobago. The little blond girl has nowhere to flee—the house in Scarsdale is too obvious and the ski condo is being rented. So the little blond girl escapes to the islands and hides in Aibileen's hutch. (Little blond girl wears Calypso macramé bikinis for the entire third act; Aibileen still wears her starched maid's outfit.) The thugs catch wind of the little blond girl's whereabouts (courtesy of a weak, coked-out friend played by Steve Buscemi) and track her to the island. In the last scene of the film, Aibileen and the little blond girl crawl behind the dunes with assault rifles and an Uzi, obliterating the bad guys as Aibileen screams at the little blond girl, "You is good, you is smart, you is important." Why couldn't that have happened to me!

Of course, with my daughters, I have overcompensated. I panic if my children DON'T crawl into bed with me in the middle of the night. In fact, I'll tiptoe into their room at 3 A.M., nudge them awake, and drag their sleepy selves down the hallway and into my bed. I tell them every day that "You is good, you is smart, you is important." And they tell me I'm not using correct grammar.

My husband and I were in Positano, Italy, savoring linguine *alle vongole* and each other when even the topless sunbathing on rocks and speedboats to Capri couldn't keep us from flying home three days early because we missed our kids. Of course when we threw our bags down and tearfully embraced them, they burst into tears because that meant the pretty babysitter had to leave.

My elder daughter had intense separation anxiety as a toddler. She would cling to my leg like a koala on a eucalyptus tree every morning at kindergarten drop-off. The teacher would plead with me to disengage and exit the classroom, but I couldn't and secretly kept her tiny fingers fastened on me. I would eventually leave (after telling my daughter I had an office right above her in the school building and had to go to work) and sit in my car and bawl. I guess I could have homeschooled her, but then today she'd only know how to bake a decent chocolate chip cookie and have watched all the episodes of *Will & Grace*. She wouldn't know math or have learned a sport. Although, based on most of reality TV now, you probably don't need much more than that to make way above minimum wage.

Let me be clear, I don't overpraise my daughters. I don't tell them they're geniuses or try to get them an audition for *Toddlers & Tiaras*. My daughters don't have tennis trophies and horseback-riding ribbons pinned all over their walls. As a parent, I don't need their success to be a reflection of me; that's a low bar. I tell them when they're mediocre or their paper on the Greek deity Artemis was "meh." I praise when it is truly warranted. When I witness them demonstrating random acts of kindness or creating a stellar Sponge Bob out of clay, I can't hide my excitement.

I also try not to emphasize their physical appearance.

They are beautiful girls, definitely more breathtaking than all the other children in the United States and most of Canada. But I don't want them to be fixated on looks. They have their father's brain and my legs and if it were the other way around, they'd be screwed.

About six months ago, I got my first "I hate you." I bet Aibileen never got one. My daughter was being impudent and as punishment I canceled a sleepover (which is easy for me because I didn't want her to leave anyway). She was so outraged she practically ripped up the wood floor with her fingernails. I said sternly, "Go to your room right now, young lady!" I felt like I was delivering a line from a TV Land sitcom. She stormed down the hallway slapping walls and pounding her Converse sneakers into the carpeting. Thankfully the apartment below is vacant or I would have gotten an eviction notice from the super.

And then I heard it, echoing down the hall: a deafening, "I hate you, Ali Wentworth!"

I willed myself not to cry. Instead, I stampeded down the hallway with such intensity, I barely missed trampling our dachshund Daisy. I kicked the door in like Jackie Chan in a Jackie Chan movie. (I assume; I've never seen one.)

"It's I hate you, MOM!" I yelled at her.

She stopped thrashing around and said, "What?"

"Don't say, 'I hate you, Ali Wentworth'—it's 'I hate you, MOM!' Please don't sully the brand!"

I lay on the sofa deep breathing after ruthlessly searching for a wine opener. And even though I knew I would endure many more years of door slamming, name-calling, and worse, in that moment I knew I had done one thing right. My daughter would not have that kind of fire if she didn't feel good, smart, and important. Well, maybe a little too important. And minutes later, she apologized in such a mature and thoughtful way. She told me she hated being at odds with me and was sorry she'd let her anger get the better of her.

She curled up against me on the couch. And as I stroked her hair and kissed her forehead I whispered, "I can't wait until we're on a desolate island and I teach you how to use a gun to assassinate bad guys."

She looked up at me with her wide eyes and whispered back, "Mom, are you drunk?"

....

CHAPTER 16

Pool of Regret

It was not until I watched my own children in action that I really comprehended the concept of sibling rivalry. When I was a kid, it was just pure survival. If my brother was coming after me with a box cutter because I cracked his Grateful Dead record, I hid in my mom's closet behind her dresses. For days if need be. When my older sister discovered a missing feather earring and came after me with an open palm, I hid in my mom's closet behind her dresses. Again. In those days punishments were sporadic and usually fell on the innocent. I had a friend in college who was one of sixteen children. When one of them stole the last of the deli meats or took the Lord's name in vain, the mother would chase the whole pack and whoever she caught would get hit with the belt. Obviously, the slow one got it the most.

I have never forgotten the time my older sister took a bullet for me. I decided, at two in the morning, to redecorate my room. I've always believed that change is good. I pulled all the books, Barbies, boxes of pens that smelled like fruit, my Wacky Pack collection, and framed photos of my dog in doll's clothing out of the bookshelves and piled them into an enormous heap in the middle of the floor. It looked like the barricade manned by the idealists in *Les Misérables*. My older sister heard the ruckus and, bleary-eyed, wandered in to see what was happening. And, unfortunately, so did my mother. My mother was so exhausted and incensed that she pulled a hairbrush from the wreckage and threatened a spanking. I was willing to succumb easily. Upon reflection, I realized I was nuts. My sister leaped in front of me with her arms extended, blocking me from our mother and her medieval weapon. "Take me, not her, take me instead," she cried. The selfless surrender confused my mother so thoroughly that she dropped the brush and went back to bed. It was a moment that still lives in me.

It pains me to witness my children fighting and telling each other they're ugly and stupid. Even more aggravating is how uninspired those insults are. Every once in a while I would like to hear, "I'm sorry I called you stupid, I thought you knew!" Or "I can explain it to you, but I can't understand it for you!" But they stick to the simple script of ugly and stupid. And even worse is when they get physical. I don't like hitting, scratching, punching, slapping, and pulling even when they tell me, "It's fine, Mom, we're just playing *The Hunger Games*."

One afternoon my children were squabbling over the last bite of Ben & Jerry's "Half Baked" ice cream. The dispute escalated into slapping and shirt pulling and I rushed to intercede. I found myself bellowing, "Don't you ever hit your sister like that! What if her temple had smacked the corner of the table? Huh? She would be brain dead! Do you want to spoon-feed her apple-sauce for the rest of your life?" Yes, extreme, but they needed to understand the concept of ramifications. And so I decided to pull a life lesson from my own personal repertoire.

When I was growing up we had a pool, the rectangular kind, with a sky blue bottom and an electronic cover. In the winter it was ignored, but by May it was the epicenter of all my parents' social soirees, everything from pool parties to stop-bys. At the end of the day our lawn would be littered with half-empty cups of iced tea and wet towels. And there was always a Barbie's head or tennis ball blocking one of the drains. My mother used to spend hours in her emerald green one-piece bathing suit straining the leaves from the water's surface with a long-handled pool net. For her it was very therapeutic.

In the spring of 1971, the pool was eerily still. There was no cacophony of shouting teenagers doing cannonballs into the chlorinated water. The household was consumed with the arrival of my younger sister, Fiona, who had been born late that April. Everything was much grander than when I entered the world. Granted, my parents' marriage was on the rocks, but photos portray my infant years in a simple existence of a sparsely decorated room with a makeshift crib and a window that overlooked an overgrown maple tree. Fiona's birth was like a royal coronation. Where I was dressed in formula-stained onesies, Fiona was adorned in long silk gowns that seemed to flow down the back of her princess crib, down the hallway, down the stairs, and down the street. There were all but animated woodland creatures singing in unison and tying pink bows around the Moses basket that held her. I watched from the stairs, my face smashed against the banister rods like a prisoner, as Fiona was toted into our house from the hospital for the first time. My stepfather held her up in the air like baby Simba in *The Lion King* for all to admire.

For the next couple of years all I heard was, "Shhhhhhh. . . . The baby is sleeping." I don't think I was allowed to touch Fiona's head for fear I might sully the crown.

It was when she was a year old and I was seven that I experienced one of the moments in life, a metaphysical fork in the road, that could have altered my life forever. I mean like *American Horror Story* altered. My mother was doing her usual pensive leaf cleaning and I was reclining on a plastic chaise longue wearing my brother's old plaid shirt and a surly attitude. Fiona was displayed on the grass in a petal pink smock dress and matching slippers. With her big blue eyes and auburn ringlets, she was the picture of perfection. She was just learning to walk and would stand up, wobble, then fall on her ruffled bloomers. I placated my crankiness by smashing ants with my thumb.

I was pondering how many grapes I could fit in my mouth without choking when Fiona, walking like a drunken uncle on Thanksgiving, grabbed the side of my chaise. She was completely focused as her brain and limbs began working in unison like baby Frankenstein. She let go and put her arms in front of her as if there were an invisible bar that would hold her up. My shark-like eyes took in her chubby little thighs and innocent adorableness. And then, as if possessed by an evil spirit, I lightly tapped my foot against the slope of her back and pushed. I watched her plummet into the water and drop like a stone. The chubby arms that had been searching for balance in the air were now groping for something to pull her up. Her eyes were closed and bubbles encircled her head. And I just watched in fascination. Like I did my lava lamp.

My mother looked over at me and dropped the net. "Where's Fiona?"

And as if she'd asked something innocuous like, "What's for lunch?" I silently and slowly pointed down toward the pool. My mother dropped the net, ran down the slate tiles, and jumped into the shallow end. Fiona shrieked loudly as my mother pulled her from the pool. My mother yelled at me as I scuttled, in shock, into the house.

Fiona was fine, but I was shaken to the core. It wasn't that I wasn't capable of such an action—it was the mindless impulse of a child—but that I never considered the consequences. My brain hadn't developed the notion of follow-through with such an impulse. As adults, of course, we know not to surrender to every subconscious whim. I don't go around sticking my tongue down every handsome stranger's mouth I see. Just to be clear, that's bad, right?

My children were silent. And frightened. I suddenly realized that sometimes life lessons have consequences too. There are consequences to consequences. However, my kids have not hit each other once since I told them the tale. In fact, they started sleeping in the same bed. And my little sister? Well, suffice it to say she's an excellent swimmer.

PART IV

Wellness

....

CHAPTER 17

Move Me

I hate exercise. It's boring, it's laborious, and it hurts. I have never experienced the infamous endorphin rush from hours of stair mastering, strenuous sex, or running through the Dakotas (North and South). Maybe if I had, I'd be a professional athlete and not sitting on my windowsill with a bag of kettle corn watching the New York Marathon. Now don't get me wrong: I like a friendly game of tennis, a relaxing swim, and I get very competitive with flashlight tag. I'm just not a gym rat.

Early in our marriage my husband used to give me fitness club subscriptions and value packs for my own trainer every Christmas. They got lost or were used to scribble grocery lists on. I've probably accumulated about sixteen thousand hours of gym time that I've never traded in. Maybe I would have a stronger, more flexible body? Maybe, but I would have missed a lot of good TV.

When I was in my early twenties I hired a trainer, Kyle, mostly because every actress I knew in Los Angeles had one. The same reason I listened to the Spice Girls. The first day Kyle had me do squats up and down my street, which, I felt, should only be reserved to torture inmates accused of securities fraud and money laundering. My knees shook, I was sweating profusely, and my ass tried to extract itself from the rest of my body and take off in my Ford Fiesta. The second day, sore and popping Advil, I asked Kyle about his love life to distract him from my imminent sit-ups. The hour went by like a shot as he regaled me with stories about his lascivious boyfriend, who was a serial cheater. He was so immersed in detailing the play-by-play in his world of gay Hollywood Adonises and their revolving door of bedmates, he didn't notice that the blue workout ball had become my pillow. For six months my money was spent curled up on my carpet listening to Kyle's stories—like sands in the hourglass, so were the gays of his life.

My thirties were devoted to Scrabble and birthing children. I may have gone skiing once or twice. And by skiing I mean I saw snow. I did have many dogs, so I must have walked a few miles? But that was the extent of my physical activity in the early part of the twenty-first century.

But something happened in my forties in the wake of two children and a preoccupation with lobster pot-pie: my body morphed. My daughters started calling me "squishy Mommy." And when my elder daughter came into my bathroom one evening and saw me standing there naked and soapy, she shrieked in horror, "I'M not going to look like that when I'm older, am I?" There was some pizza dough dangling from the wrong places, and if I reached up high to get a wineglass my midsection resembled those neck pillows you buy in the airport for long flights. So, okay, I was not tight. But the last thing I wanted to do was forbid myself cheese fondue, home-made bread, and raw cookie dough. I love food. I spend afternoons dreaming about dinner—a burger with ched-dar and bacon, maybe linguine with clams, and grilled peaches with cinnamon ice cream. Just for example. I could never give up dairy and sugar and gluten. I don't even know what gluten is, but I know I love it.

So that left exercise. I can't tell you how many moms drop off their kids at school in their spandex leggings and Nike tank tops and say to each other, "As long as I do Pilates and forty-five minutes of cardio, I can eat whatever I want." Pilates and forty-five minutes of car-dio? They elect to do that? They choose pain over apple cider doughnuts and *Live with Kelly and Michael*? But the fact remained that if I was going to eat like a linebacker, I had to compensate with movement.

The icing on the lemon poppy seed cake with cream cheese frosting was my annual physical evaluation with my internist. "You've lost a lot of muscle mass," she informed me seconds into the examination.

"Does that mean I'm thinner?" I smiled.

She paused for a moment and then quite sternly asked me, "Do you have a living will?"

I was so depressed walking home from the doctor's office I had to stop at Magnolia Bakery and inhale two red velvet cupcakes. I realized that exercise was no longer about looking svelte in a sleeveless shirt; it was about not losing my balance, falling down, breaking a hip, and becoming immobile for the rest of my life. I spent the rest of the afternoon on the National Institute of Aging Web site.

In the past, the only time my body had been fit and firm was when I was depressed. I wouldn't eat and walked around in circles all night biting my nails. But you can't conjure up a bout of depression. I even begged my husband to leave me for a couple of years and when I was down to my fighting weight, come back. He thought there was an easier way to get healthy.

I finally decided to find a fitness regimen and avoid my demise. This meant asking my hale and vigorous friends what their exercise routines looked like. I fig-

ured I would test-drive a few before I found "the one."
You know, like dating.

My friend Lana has a sinewy body with stretchy limbs
and limber legs. A look I coveted. And so I went to my
first yoga class. Not the hot Bikram yoga, where everyone excretes all their nasty toxins and fluids in your face
and a fart becomes a napalm bomb, but the light and
breezy yoga as portrayed on Caribbean spa brochures.

I bought accessories, naturally: soft billowy white
yoga pants and cotton tank tops with little printed Bud-
dhas on them and a lime green mat with a lavender lo-
tus. This was just my speed: comfy clothes, no weights,
and no loud music. Maybe even a nap. Namaste.

I sat Indian style on my mat as younger women with
loose braids and armpit hair descended onto the maple-
wood floor. There was lots of stretching and breathing
and toe cracking. An intense aroma awakened my gag
reflex and I assumed it was some hideous musk incense
to ward off evil spirits only to realize that the dude
wearing a shark tooth necklace next to me who looked
like Jesus Christ had submerged himself in a bucket of
patchouli oil. This proved difficult during the inhaling
portion of the program. It's times like these when I wish
my vagina would pitch in and do some of the breathing.

Yoga was not for me, I decided quickly. It was too
passive. I realized I did need disco music and an Olivia
Newton-John–looking lady in leg warmers to jump up

and down and scream, "Let's get physical!" Was there such a thing as disco yoga? I pretended I had to pee when we were told to touch our toes (I can barely touch my knees) and left the class and my mat forever. It, however, wasn't a total loss; I still sleep in the yoga clothes.

For years I tried to subscribe to the adage "I'll have what she's having" when it came to Gwyneth Paltrow. I don't have the patience to keep my blond hair that buttery hue and the cleansing ritual strikes me as running the risk of expelling vital organs, but her body . . . I figured we were the same age (give or take a decade) and that perhaps she was on to something when it came to having a champion physique. At the time she was doing two hours of intense cardio (based on videos on her Web site goop). Well, I thought, I can do that! It's just dancing! And dancing is fun! Who doesn't like dancing? I called a dance instructor who taught ballet, swing, and weight-loss salsa on Thursdays at the YMCA. As you can tell, I approach fitness the way most women approach a haircut. Some women tear out a photo of Meg Ryan in a magazine and take it to the salon: "I want that cut." I tear a photo of Gisele Bündchen out of the *Sports Illustrated* swimsuit edition and say, "I want that bod."

The first day of my physical metamorphosis I wore biker shorts and a cross-back sports top that took me two hours to put on. I was certain having one boob exposed and the other boob half matted down by a strap wasn't right. Nicole, my instructor, also wore little black biker shorts and a neon pink midriff halter top. She was *Maxim* magazine hot; I was Zumba instructor from Maine hot. Nicole was pure muscle. A ravenous cannibal would throw her back. She'd be the last human eaten on the snowy mountain crash site. I'd be third.

We entered the pristine gym. It was a sauna. The heat was turned up to 90 degrees to get the sweat glands pumping. My sweat glands dried up like raisins. Nicole started jumping up and down like a toddler cracked out on Skittles. The speakers blared Keisha as Nicole screamed, "Yeah," and "Woo!"

After a few sideways vines, I felt like I was going to black out. Nicole immediately stopped the music and escorted me outside for some fresh air. You would have thought it was bring your great-grandmother to work day. She looked with terror at my splotchy purple face; clearly she had never experienced anyone so close to expiration. "You okay? We've only worked out for one and a half minutes."

My head was between my legs and I poured a bottle of water down my neck. We sat on the grass for about twenty minutes until my color was back to its natural light gray. "Shall we go back?"

How dare she push me so hard; I wasn't training for

the Olympics. "Okay," I said, "but can we turn off the heat?"

"Sure."

"And maybe change the music?"

Nicole thought if we danced it would awaken many of the muscles in my thighs that had never been used before. I was like a baby colt learning to walk.

"You're going to turn, turn, sashay, and kick," Nicole sang. I had a posttraumatic flashback of taking (failing) tap in acting school. I was always in the back of the class doing my best Gene Kelly impression, just without the grace, talent, or skill. I shuffled up to the wall of mirrors and back toward the door. Twice. Then sashayed out the door to throw up in the parking lot. I think Nicole thought I had a terminal disease. As I wiped my mouth with a wet wipe, I waved the white flag.

"Okay, I get it, but the first day is always tough; I'll see you Friday!" she said and smiled. That was the last time I ever saw Nicole. Now when I see a photo of Gwyneth Paltrow in a magazine looking physically impeccable, I know firsthand the work and sweat it took to get that way. I wonder if she thinks the same about me?

"Oh my God, I am OBSESSED with SoulCycle!" Gillian must have said twenty times during lunch. "It's so fun, you forget you're even working out!" And that was the tag line I had been waiting for. The only better endorsement would be, "You don't even know you're exercising because you're asleep the whole time!" I remember hearing a myth that in the 1950s women would be put under general anesthesia when they went into labor and upon awakening, found themselves cleaned, stitched, hair blown out, and cradling a baby. There must be a way to do that with exercise?

SoulCycle has a line of clothing that I had to peruse before fully committing. It took me all of four minutes to purchase some Soul Sweat capris and a hologram skull Soul tank. I met Gillian at the sought-after class in midtown Manhattan. Apparently SoulCycle instructors have a hierarchy of popularity based on their enthusiasm and playlist. I even heard rumors of wealthy hedge fund wives who left their paunchy husbands for glistening female instructors with big guns. I have a striking friend who loses her impetus to sweat if the lady instructor doesn't flirt with her.

Well, yoga may have been too passive, but SoulCycle was too aggressive. I can't enter a dark room with booming disco rap without my roller skates and jazz hands. I was not just intimidated: I was frightened. When I mounted the bike, the seat hit my vagina bone in such a way that it caused the kind of painful jolt only felt once before in sixth grade art class when I rammed into the corner of the art table and thought I'd lost my virginity. I waved to Gillian to carry on, dismounted, and disappeared into the lobby. I walked home like a wounded cowgirl.

When I got back to the apartment, I crawled onto my heating pad in my bed with the rest of my Juice Press chocolate protein smoothie I felt I'd earned. I decided to make an exercise list in order to prune my choices:

1. Aerobics: I have a heart murmur.
2. Ballet: too old.
3. Baseball: need a team.
4. Basketball: too short.
5. Biking: bulbous vagina.
6. Boating: need a boat.
7. Bowling: need a league.
8. Boxing: those girls scare me.
9. Canoeing: in Manhattan?
10. Football: soft skull.
11. Frisbee: not without pot and a black Lab.
12. Golf: if I didn't have kids. And a life.
13. Gymnastics: only in bed.
14. Hiking: blech.
15. Horseback riding: need a horse.
16. Hula hooping: flatulent.
17. Ice-skating: bad knees (but love the clothes).
18. Jogging: never.
19. Juggling: why not jousting?
20. Jump rope: uncoordinated.
21. Laser tag: Huh?
22. Ping-Pong: if I sell the dining room table.

23. Rock climbing: vertigo.
24. Roller skating: at the *Playboy* mansion?
25. Running: over my dead body.
26. Skiing: only in the lodge.
27. Swimming: green hair.
28. Tae Kwon Do: don't speak Chinese.
29. Tennis: that elbow thing.
30. Trampoline: vomit.
31. Walking: have to leave something for eighty.
32. Weight lifting: I'm straight.

I slurped the last vestiges of chocolate shavings at the bottom of my cup. I was proud of myself. I had thoroughly gone through all the physical options and, as it turned out, was not suitable for any of them. Like mustard and strawberry jam, exercise and I were not the right match.

I recently renamed one of our dachshunds "Six Miles." So now at school pick-up I just say, "I walk six miles every day!"

CHAPTER 18

....

Ch-ch-ch-changes

I bet you've never received this phone call—"Oh, hi!
Listen, a Japanese pharmaceutical company is interested in having you host a panel for their new postmenopausal dry-vagina cream to combat painful sex."
Or maybe you have. My first response was to feel flat-
tered that somebody wanted me for anything, let alone
to host a panel. Then I was horrified to realize that they
assumed I was potentially postmenopausal (for the record: as of the time of publication, I haven't even reached
perimenopause). And third, and most distressing, was
the concept that at that later stage, sex is painful? Sex is
painful at the beginning of one's sexual life, but also at
the end? I decided to take the job for three important

reasons: I wanted to know more; they were paying me; and there was a chance I could get my hands on that cream for future needs. But really, they were paying me.

I find menopause incredibly unfair. Why do women need a physical metamorphosis to trumpet to the world that they are no longer nubile and capable of procreating? Nothing happens to men! Why don't their balls dry up and fall off like acorns in autumn? I also don't like the idea that once we're no longer capable of producing offspring we should just let ourselves go and take jewelry-making classes. But again, I'm fortyish with the ovaries of a teenager.

I shuddered at the thought of discussing sex and vaginas in such a public forum. We never discussed sex growing up. Everything was learned on *Animal Kingdom* or via rambling misinformation from a few dimwits at an all-girls school. (I would be in my early thirties when I discovered that a gang bang was not a dance-off between two groups of inner city thugs.)

I remember one Christmas Eve my mother and I stayed up late to stuff stockings. We were filling knitted socks with English chocolates and clementines. I was flitting about the tree with homemade popcorn and cranberry strings. My mother hummed along with "Oh, Come, All Ye Faithful" as it flowed in from the kitchen radio. Feeling a surge of endearment, I turned to her. "How come growing up we never discussed masturbation?" There was dead silence but for the sound of a tiny orange dropping. It rolled for an interminable amount of time down the wood-plank floor before hitting the fireplace screen. She continued humming. And that pretty much sums up the whole sexual education of my youth.

The moment you have children, your sex drive seesaws between that of a sex-crazed Jezebel and a chaste Mother Superior. On the one hand, any hormonal surge can make you "hungry like a wolf" (I have heard of, but not personally experienced, this phenomenon occurring right after childbirth). But the opposite response—the equivalent of hanging up a "gone fishing" sign below— could be the result of a fetus the size of a canary melon torpedoing through your loins, resulting in a week of sanitary napkins and granny pants. Or perhaps the fact that a human being is suckling on your tit, stretching it down to your belly button. Or it could just be sleep deprivation that inspires you to eat cereal over the sink and let your armpit hair grow into dreadlocks. Take your pick.

By the time you're back in the sexual saddle, your children have grown into walking and talking libido stompers. The recurring nightmare that sends them whimpering into your bed every night and thrashing their arms in your face becomes your recurring nightmare that you will never have sex again. On a related note: our dachshund, Gilbert, insisted on burrowing

under our duvet and nestling right between my husband's feet and my own. If my husband moved in a way
that so much as suggested an incoming kiss, Gilbert
would growl so ferociously, we would hasten back to
our opposite sides of the bed. My husband wasn't the
only one neutered.

Nothing questions your outlook on sexuality like
one's own offspring on the brink of puberty. This past
spring my fifth-grader's school had a full immersion into
the study and understanding of puberty and sexual re-
production. Now, in the olden days, we were taught
with a tattered anatomical chart that had the genitals
highlighted in primary colors. There was a diagram of
a penis in various stages, from the flaccid to semierect
and then erect positions. I thought the man in the chart
had three penises (imagine the terror). And the fallopian
tubes and ovaries looked like chicken livers. It was all
very clinical and pleasure was never mentioned. But in
this age of Internet porn, social media, and *Gossip Girl,*
the antiseptic approach to sex ed does not suffice. It is
no longer just the birds and the bees—now, the bird
embarks on a relationship with the bee, realizes he's gay,
and goes back to a bird only to find out she's transgen-
dering into a beetle.

I almost choked on a turkey meatball when my
daughter innocently blurted out during family dinner,
"Do you guys have anal sex?"

I instantly transformed into a ninety-year-old woman from *Footloose,* with a lace doily around my neck, a wicker purse, and a Bible. "Is THAT what they're teaching you at school?"

She was startled. "Mom, there's all kinds of sex; there's straight sex, gay sex . . . you know Laney has two dads!"

My younger daughter is privy to some of these inquisitions but hasn't taken in what it all means. One afternoon we were unwrapping new bedding for the girls' room; as she ripped the plastic off some mattress pads she innocently asked, "Are these for wet dreams?"

I softly answered, "No, sweetie, mildew."

And now back to my future painful postmenopausal sex. Was I up for the task of openly discussing it? Did I have my own vagina monologue? And was I the only actress they could get?

I was greeted on the twenty-first floor of a midtown hotel by a gaggle of young, fertile women in Club Monaco attire. They held clipboards and asked me if I needed to use the bathroom, wanted bottled water, or required some privacy before the panel began. I shyly told them I was fine and pretended to be busy on my cell phone. I clicked away as if I was in the middle of a Viacom deal, but was really perusing my kids' Instagrams. I stole looks at the crowd filling the cool, retro space that overlooked the Upper West Side. Who would come to a panel about postmenopausal dry vaginas? Well, magazine health editors, bloggers, and the press. And a slightly bald, paunchy man who I think got off on the wrong floor, saw the cheese and cracker spread, and decided to stay. You should have seen his face when I opened the evening with, "I welcome you, but more important, my vagina welcomes you." I think he may have bitten his finger off.

The other panelists consisted of two highly reputable doctors who specialize in menopause and a sex therapist. They were attractive, brilliant women who were earning their Ph.D.s at the same time I was auditioning to be on *One Life to Live*. They were poised and completely comfortable discussing the medical remedies for the thinning and less flexible vagina. Many unappealing words were bandied about—irrational, moody, depressed, exhaustion, weepy, weight gain, dry skin, hair loss, and sleeplessness. And I countered with hackneyed jokes about "dry" humor and vaginoplasty. I was hired as entertainment, not for my biochemical expertise, so I did feel compelled to be more Don Rickles than Dr. Oz.

In the middle of the event, however, there was a shift. I started asking genuine questions about what my sexual future looked like. What caught my attention was the term "atrophic vaginitis." Wasn't atrophy the wasting away of a body part? So my vagina was going to waste away? What would be left? I probably should have moved the event along, but I was dumbfounded. My whole body became atrophic! Oh, how naive I had been about menopause. I thought one just had night sweats and threw plates. We were suddenly discussing the breakdown of the vaginal lining because of lack of estrogen and mucus. And painful intercourse! I mean, seriously, how much pain are we talking?

After the event I collected the doctors' contacts like they were Major League baseball cards at a sports exchange expo. Women from the audience came up and thanked me for "starting the conversation." I felt like my generation's Betty Friedan. Wait, is she my generation?

For weeks after the panel I was the postmenopause dry-vagina expert among my friends. I would take walks, meet for drinks, or hang in the park at play dates educating my ladies on what to expect. They are all depressed now. But don't kill the messenger, right? Like an old Jewish woman I keep saying with my finger pointed, "Estrogen, estrogen, estrogen!"

I've never paid much attention to my sexual health. As long as I didn't have an STD or I was pregnant when I wanted to be, I didn't take notice. I hadn't realized that sexuality had so many different peaks and valleys. All I knew was that we start in diapers and end in them. I just pray that after menopause there's another sexual renaissance. After all, there has to be more to do than just play gin rummy.

On a side note: I did receive a box of the postmenopausal dry-vagina cream. I plan on using it in my promotional book giveaway.

....

CHAPTER 19

Going for the Bronze

When I was a kid, I owned a rock tumbler. I would find stones and bits of rough gravel, drop them in the machine, and set it churning until the rocks fell out smooth and sparkling. Oh, how shiny and beautiful they were, nothing like the rocks that went in!

I believe there is an undisclosed, covert human polish machine in Hollywood accessible only to A-list celebrities. There is a sheen and silky glow to women like Jennifer Lopez and Angelina Jolie not found in the women I see at school drop-off, at Whole Foods, or in line at the DMV. How could I obtain access to such a magical churner that would burnish me into a semiprecious Sharon Stone? I have read all the blogs and studied beauty notes in magazines at the colorist, but soaking my hair in olive oil and doing leg presses with a huge rubber band wrapped around my knees while I watch *Homeland* just doesn't seem to leave me with that same luminousness. I'm still indistinct rubble.

I have heard all kinds of whispers about such things as human growth hormones, snake venom, and pig placenta being the special sauce for eternal youth in Hollywood. I'm not interested in pursuing these methods mostly because I'm petrified of snakes and wouldn't know the first thing about extracting venom. As a drag queen friend of mine once said, "Gurl, if I ever ran into a snake I'd be so scared I'd drop a litter!" And pig placenta can't smell good. I could never take human growth hormones mostly because I'd be afraid I'd Benjamin-Button back to infancy. And then I would have to take the SATs again. So I take what's accessible to me, in my price range, and won't involve a body scrub made from armadillo liver.

I know spray tan has been around since pre–Suzanne Somers, but it seems the industry has progressed and you no longer have to lie flat while hundreds of small children hand-paint you with umber oils. A few women had told me that spray tanning makes you darker, thinner, younger, richer, and happier. . . .

I can't do the tanning bed. For one, it's so 1970s. And two, I would have to dedicate way too much time in that claustrophobic capsule wearing white plastic swim goggles. With the amount of time I would have to commit to the tanning bed, well, I could go mulch some trees or get a mammogram, maybe read to my kids!

It was one afternoon at the beach that I decided to take my pale exterior to the next shade. Sunbathing leaves me a rosy pink, slightly sun-poisoned hue, not a Mediterranean bronze. And I'm married to a Greek who even in a rainstorm will get Tootsie Roll brown. So I asked the pretty college girl, who I buy my Carvel Cookie Puss cakes from, where I could get me one of those so-called spray tans. I couldn't tell if she was insulted or complimented when she answered, "You mean fake tan? I'm tan 'cause I'm a lifeguard. And it's summer!" Every year I loathe young people even more.

I Googled salons with names like Glowjob until I found one located near me and swiftly made an appointment. I wasn't sure what to wear to the salon. Do I wear my one-piece Speedo? A bikini? The bikini bottom? Do I wear a robe to the salon? That would mean I'd have to drive, park, and walk the sidewalk in a robe, which could result in an arrest.

When I asked the question I pose when facing all major quandaries in my life—what would Julia Roberts do?—I settled on a sundress. I entered the salon and whispered to the receptionist, "I'm here for a spray tan," as if I was scoring amphetamines on the down low.

I was escorted by a sweet non-English-speaking woman down the stairs, bypassing huge vats of peroxide and boxes of rubber gloves. It seemed the hair and makeup were allowed to flourish upstairs on full display, but the nasty little business of fake tanning and hair removal had to be executed below in the catacombs. As we passed the waxing room, I could hear the screams.

We entered a nook the size of a Porta-Potty. The lady, like a disheartened mime, gestured for me to get undressed. I snapped my underwear to imply "Keep on, yes?" which was met with a slightly hostile look of "No, you idiot, get naked, I've seen 'em all."

She stepped out of the nook, giving me a chance to strip. I was surrounded by black garbage bags taped to every inch of the tiny wall space. I was a porno puppet preparing for the matinee.

When the lady came back in, she inspected my body with intense scrutiny. I blurted out, "I know, I had pneumonia, so I haven't worked out in a long time . . ." She didn't care or understand me. She was just trying to figure out what color to spray my chicken flesh. She then did something I have not experienced since elementary school gymnastics; she powdered my palms and the flats of my feet. Was there a dismount I was not aware of? I suppose tan palms are a dead giveaway for artificial coloring. (A good reason to not take tanning pills, which contain massive amounts of beta-carotene and will turn every skin cell bright Oompa Loompa orange.)

Suddenly, the hose and sprayer turned on with the thundering sound of a car wash. I closed my eyes and thought of Meryl Streep in the film *Silkwood* getting power washed to eradicate any nuclear particles. And I suddenly felt sorry for my poor dogs because I inflict this hose torture on them regularly. I swore from that moment on I would only bathe them in a warm tub with elixirs that smelled like bacon.

I was signaled to stand to the side by a slight flick of her hand on my shoulder. And then to the back. And then to the other side. Somehow it was more humiliating than getting a real mug shot. I'm not squeamish about being naked. God knows my daughters can tell you that. But it's hard not to feel exposed when an older woman is inches away from your vagina holding a pistol and spraying it like it's infested with roaches.

When she was finished, she eyeballed her work like a surgeon. I was asked to turn around once more as she squirted hidden areas (yes, creases). And then came the money shot. And for this one position I gave her a 50 percent tip. She signaled for me to turn around and face the wall while parting my buttocks. I laughed. She saw no humor. I pantomimed bending over and spreading my cheeks. Yes, she nodded. I gestured, "Oh, that's okay, I'm good!" Who would be so close to my ass to see that my intergluteal cleft (or crack) wasn't tan? But she wasn't having it. She was quite serious. You'd think I asked Cezanne to just paint the apples and forget the oranges. And so I dipped down, exposing the area where, ironically, the sun never shines. I even held my breath for no good reason.

As she used a damp sponge to blend any streaks, I found myself wondering if I could hire her to stain my wood floors. The lady placed the hose back in its holster. She gesticulated that I should stand with my arms spread for a few minutes. And then added, "Stay here," which I'm glad she did because otherwise I'm sure I would have just bounced upstairs buck naked and searched for the new *Glamour* magazine. So there I stood. Talk about watching paint dry!

I purposely refrained from eyeing the mirror behind the door. There was no need for any further degradation. My mind knows how to wander in most idle situations—in the dentist's waiting room, on the subway, during sex . . . but at that moment, standing there nude in a tiny, black plastic nook, my brain settled on the film *Taken* starring Liam Neeson. In the film he plays a detective who rescues his daughter from some sex-trafficking bad guys who have kidnapped her. I recalled the scene where the daughter (drugged out) had to stand in lingerie in front of a bunch of thugs during a sex slave auction. And at that moment, I totally understood what that daughter was going through. And then I wondered, if I was ever kidnapped by an international sex-trafficking ring, would my father fly to Paris, figure out what yacht I was imprisoned on, kill the band of assassins, and rescue me? And I decided he would. After all, I never thought of Liam Neeson as an action star before that movie and the same could be said for my dad. By the time my lady returned, I was comforted in knowing that if I were ever in that position— particularly as a middle-aged woman prone to yeast infections—I would be saved.

I got dressed carefully. I didn't want my new café au lait skin to rub off on my floral dress. The paint had a distinct chemical smell, like turpentine, and my skin felt sticky, like someone had rubbed a Butterfinger all over me.

I walked through the city trying to make eye contact with passersby in the hopes of hearing, "Hey, Ali"— well, they wouldn't know me so—"Hey, woman! Look at your glow! You've really got it going on!"

But nothing. Not so much as a glance. And when I picked up my kids from camp? Nada. Even when I told them I had a spray tan, they inspected me and then accused me of lying. I mean, of all the things I could lie to them about, they pick a spray tan? They never questioned that TV only works in the rain? Or good things only happen to good people?

I woke up the next morning under the delusion that somehow overnight the paint had penetrated my derma more deeply and I would rise as a Tahitian princess. I wasn't cadaverous, but just as pale as the day I was born. What did get tan? My new Yves Delorme sheets I scored on Gilt.com! They were smeared in orange, as if Jackson Pollock had designed them for Macy's. I picked up my sundress from the day before (yes, it was on the floor, it was a Saturday) and it was as if someone had murdered a tangerine.

So maybe I will never have access to the miraculous and mysterious polishing machine. Maybe you need a platinum record or a Golden Globe to be granted such a pass. Otherwise, how would we sell magazines, clothing, cosmetics, and dreams? You often hear people say about movie stars, "Well, it's their job to be gorgeous!" And maybe that's true. I'm predominately a mom. So perhaps it's my job to display the appropriate battle wounds. It is my job to have cellulite, age spots, stretch marks, ingrown toenails—and turkey meatballs on the table at 6 P.M. Let Charlize Theron try to do that!

CHAPTER 20

....

Not the Face

I was curled up on my sofa with my mug (which has a picture of Lionel Richie on it and says HELLO? IS IT TEA YOU'RE LOOKING FOR?) filled with PG Tips and loads of cream watching *Good Morning America* when I suddenly spewed liquid all over my pajamas. On national television, Lena Dunham, award-winning actress, writer, director, voice of a generation, and a woman I admire, called my husband "a sexual icon." A SEXUAL ICON! Well, I figured, it was just a matter of time before he left me. He would have his pick of every twenty-something Brooklyn-based, braless, offbeat girl. Yes, with all the tattoos and piercings, the odds were pretty high that he would contract

·205·

hepatitis C. But they are all so coquettish and verbally raw, I don't think he'd mind.

Well, that's it, I decided, I was getting Botox.

Have I mentioned that I'm terrified of needles? Whenever a nurse takes my blood, I latch on to her waist like a needy toddler and have at least three other medical administrators sing a Taylor Swift song or describe their first kiss. And I always scream like they are extracting organs without numbing cream. Yes, I am a doctor's worst nightmare. I can't even watch my children get shots. They can't fathom why their mother is running down the hall, bawling, before the alcohol has even been rubbed. I don't get flu shots; I get flu nasal snorts. Apparently, after age fifty you have to get the shot. Reason enough to lie about my age for the next twenty years.

Beyond my needle phobia, there is the fact that Botox is a lethal toxin. I was contemplating injecting a life-threatening illness into my body to paralyze facial muscles. Oh, what the hell, I wanted to be pretty.

I wasn't sure how to find a Botox doctor. Walk up to strange women on the street and ask, "Hey, who did your face?" I started looking through magazines at people whose faces I coveted and that looked real enough. I figured I could call their agents or publicists? Oh, right, celebrities don't have any "work done." They just drink a lot of water or are happy in their current relationship.

I have a friend, Ruthie, whom I've known for twenty years. A witty and warm woman who makes me wish I were born a Jew. She is currently teaching me Yiddish. I should be fluent by Hanukkah. Well, luckily, she's married to a Park Avenue doctor! Not only a doctor, but a plastic surgeon—the good kind. Like I would know from a good plastic surgeon! I called her and asked if her husband, Ezra, dabbled in Botox. "Are you kidding me? Why do you think he looks twenty? He injects the leftovers on himself!"

I explained my aversion to needles, but that I needed to do something before my husband ran off with Lena Dunham.

"Are you nuts? Your husband is a mensch, he will never leave you, even if you lost your whole face."

"I know," I said, "but now he's a sexual icon."

"Ah, yeah, that's a tough one. I tell you what, I've never had Botox either, and my looks are going to the dogs; I'll go with you!"

I figured since she was married to the guy, we wouldn't have a six-month wait.

I had no idea what Botox cost. Did you pay by the prick? By the ounce or bag like drugs? It could have been ten dollars or five hundred. But I figured I would get the friends and family rate. After all, I went to their son's bar mitzvah and I don't mean just the party—temple too.

The office was in the East Sixties on Park Avenue. This area is the mecca of medical hotshots. I think because it's the Upper East Side, people assume that if the doctor can afford the rent, he must be exemplary. I mean, would you get a butt lift in Coney Island? I just didn't want to end up with a droopy eye or missing an ear.

The waiting room could have been my grandmother's Chicago living room circa 1968. There was a worn chenille sofa and two oak chairs with ornately carved arms, a coffee table with a toile tray covered in two-year-old magazines, and a fern (which I suspect was fake). I was devouring a pamphlet on Juvéderm when Ruthie stomped into the room. "Oy! Are we sure we want to do this? I couldn't sleep all night!"

Oh, there was no turning back now. I have jumped out of a plane and walked nude on a public beach, so injecting botulism into my forehead for the sake of keeping my husband was definitely within the realm of possibility. I would take a needle for him.

My favorite thing about Ruthie and her husband, Dr. Ezra, is that when they're together they morph into a pair of Borscht Belt comedians. In the 1950s they would have done warm-up for Shecky Greene. When Ezra led us into the inner sanctum of tummy tucks and breast enhancements, Ruthie began to balk. *"Oy gevalt!"*

I watched Ezra fill the syringe with the evil potion.

"You hear my wife kvetching?" he chuckled. I stared at the clear serum. My armpits started to emit a scent associated with high-stress situations like public speaking and parent-teacher conferences.

Ruthie started pacing. "This is *fercockt,* look at that needle! I'm about to *plotz!*"

Ezra, slightly annoyed, rolled his eyes at me. "You hear all this *tummel*? I'm about to punch her in her *kishka!*"

My palms started to sweat; who would go first? Did I get it over with? Or did I watch Ruthie suffer so I could get a better grasp of the situation and see how much blood was involved? I could always escape out the back (or entrance, for incognito famous people) if it was a nip/tuck horror show.

Ezra made the choice for me. "Ali, you go and show this *pisher* what's what!" He slapped on the rubber gloves and I lay back in his teal blue pleather medical chair. I closed my eyes and willed myself to take it like a man, or woman, take it like a Kardashian. Ezra hit a pedal and the chair slowly and loudly reclined.

"*Bissela, bissela,*" Ruthie shouted.

I opened my eyes. "What's *bissela*?" I had to make sure it didn't mean wrong place, wrong place!

Ezra stopped, turned, and gave Ruthie a look as a droplet fell off the tip of the needle onto the floor. He turned back to me; my jaw was clenched. "It means a little."

I took a deep breath and went to my quiet place. I could feel the needle pinch and then penetrate the skin. Once by my left brow, then my right. My eyes were tearing. And I hadn't exhaled. Then a sharp pinch between the furrow in my brows. Just as his fingers ran along the sides of my eyes—well, crow's-feet—I barked, "I'm good!" I had visions of my face distorting like a Modigliani painting.

My outburst sent Ruthie into a panic. "What? What? You okay . . . Ezra, something's wrong? What have you done, you *alter cocker*?" Ezra was unfazed. When Ruthie's grocery delivery is thirty minutes late, she calls 911. He handed me a bag of ice and pressed it on my forehead. The freeze hurt more than the injections.

"Oy!" Ruthie inspected my face. "She looks like she got stung by a hive of bees!"

I kept checking in the mirror to see if I had transformed into Jessica Biel. It was still just me, but with red bumps.

Ezra was wrestling Ruthie into the chair while I continued to numb my *punim* (that's Yiddish for face) with the ice pack. I had to side with Ezra a little; Ruthie was acting like she was being tied to a head crusher.

"Listen to me, listen to me . . . *bissela, bissela*!" Ezra pointed to his wife. "You see this? I'm giving her free Botox, something my clients pay hundreds of dollars for, and look at her? Like I'm pulling out all her teeth!"

"Come on, I don't have the *koyakh,* give me the damn juice!" Thank God I went first. Watching Ruthie was like being in the front row of a beheading.

We sat in the waiting room with ice packs on our foreheads, clinging to the fern and moaning like two old German shepherds with hip dysplasia. Ezra chuckled as he opened a box of gelatinous implants.

I lifted my throbbing head. "Ezra, how much do I owe you? Does Cigna Health cover this?"

He slammed a double D on the desk. "Don't be ridiculous! You're *mishpacha*! You pay me nothing."

I'm not comfortable with owing people. I believe a service should be reciprocated with money or sex, preferably money. "Ezra, please, let me pay you something! Or clean your office?"

Ruthie continued moaning. "I can't feel my brain!"

"Ali, I tell you what, you bake me some of those chocolate chip cookies and we'll call it even." Yes, they're THAT good!

"No! No cookies! Ezra, we don't need any more sweets in the house. I can't fit into any of my pants!"

He smiled. "Why? I do lipo!"

I negotiated a box of cookies and a dozen brownies that I would hand-deliver to his office the next day.

Ruthie and I walked up Park Avenue, periodically

checking out each other's facades. For ten blocks all I heard was, "Is it bruised? It's bruised, isn't it? Oy, that quack."

We finally parted at Seventy-eighth Street. Ruthie had to speak with her super; there were accusations floating around her building that her shih tzu had bitten one of the doormen.

As I continued walking I thought about the pain of beauty and all the women who try to mask their age, only to be outdone by their necks, which always give it away. And the price of upkeep: I would have to do a lot of baking. I wondered what a dozen whoopee pies would get me? Would I even get Botox again?

And then it dawned on me: I was so fixated on myself, I had forgotten to stop at the drugstore and pick up dandruff shampoo for the sexual icon.

CHAPTER 21

···

Is That All There Is?

I don't know why I burst into tears, but I did. I was weeping driving down Sunset Boulevard past strip clubs, the Viper Room, and the Roxy, looking for a juice bar or smoothie hut or someplace to sip something sweet to rid my mouth of last night's melatonin metallic taste. Every time I stopped at a light, I would catch the guy in the Lamborghini with the license plate—MOGUL— eyeing my hysteria. I pretended I was on speakerphone, laughing. The window was down, so I kept repeating, "You kill me, Louis CK!" I'd been in Los Angeles less than twenty-four hours on a pitching spree. Which means I fly out on my own dime with some half-baked television idea in the hopes that I sell the script, they make it into a show, that show goes into syndication, and I eventually feel like an empowered female. And that feeling propels me to finally start exercising. It's amusing the places I go to feel accomplishment. And it's not the same fulfillment as watching your child ride a bike for the first time or ladling corn chowder at a soup kitchen. It's not selfless. It's more of a "See? I'm not such a loser, I too can be in the *Hollywood Reporter* as a player [pronounced 'playa']." Oh, I'm not proud of the feeling, but I have to acknowledge it because it is the feeling that got me in the rental car cruising down Sunset Boulevard in the first place! But why the sobbing?

The last time I was truly single was when I lived in the Hollywood Hills. I was young (well, any age is young to me now), a bachelorette, and every day was full of the possibility of fortuitousness and action. A movie deal, starring in a TV show, and making out with Channing Tatum were all just a whiff away. There was always a meeting or an audition that could instantly blast me into the stratosphere of celebrity. Or there was some creative pal to meet with and discuss a provocative idea based on a *New Yorker* cartoon over sake at a Rock'N Sushi happy hour. But that was then. Today, I am very married, a mother, and the odds of the barometer of my life moving in any significant way are slight at best.

I was on my way to the valley via Laurel Canyon, a mecca of cliff-side, stucco hippie crash pads, the tree houses of wayward actors, and a little general store that blares Rasta music. I always experience a jolt coming over the peak of the canyons, where a deeply tanned homeless man is skateboarding and there's a pungent smell of marijuana and jasmine over to the valley, which is essentially an endless line of mini-malls and frozen yogurt shacks. How much Pinkberry, Bigg Chill, Humphreys, Menchie's, and Yogurtland can these people devour? They must have extremely healthy colony-forming units of microorganisms based on the enormous amounts of lactobacillus they consume. And gas.

The San Fernando Valley is always ten degrees hotter, which makes me ten degrees sadder. I was en route to pitch to two networks. And a vast majority of corporate television lives in the dry climate of the San Fernando desert. Yes, television executives and rattlesnakes.

In between being paraded into spare conference rooms, where I tried to convince executives with glazed-over eyes that my genius idea for a multicamera sitcom would be bigger than *Cheers* and more lucrative than *Modern Family,* I would sit on a velveteen sofa from Overstock.com in the waiting area and ponder why I didn't live in London and own a sublimely lit gallery in Hoxton Square that featured the works of Lucian Freud. I made clear to my audience, slugging down their coffee lattes, that my success would validate their need for bigger Spanish-style mansions closer to the beach and shinier Mercedes.

There was something disheartening about slogging up the hill in my rented SUV now, some twenty years later, with the same old bag of tricks, jokes, and need for approval. I was even older than the executives I was pitching. And those kinds of feelings are a punch in the stomach worse than sex in a strange position.

But my melancholy ran deeper than a simple case of capitalist malaise. My closest girlfriends still reside in L.A. They're not in the minuscule tenements of their twenties committed only to their rescue pit bull mixes; now they throw soccer balls on their lush lawns in Santa Monica in front of their chalky white, four-bedroom haciendas covered in fuchsia bougainvillea. They are constant reminders of my past life in L.A., although they too have aged. They haven't frozen in time (well, maybe their foreheads) and are a reminder that I too am getting older and worried about retirement funds and whether to put teenagers on Ritalin. A visit to L.A. these days is as depressingly nostalgic as riding It's a Small World at Disneyland—instead of feeling over-whelmed by the magnificence, I find myself focusing on the air-conditioning vents on the ceilings amidst painted clouds.

As I cruised by a dilapidated shack in the hills, I re-called once making out with the guy who lived there before it was condemned. He was a South American retro furniture dealer with his own shop in Hollywood. I had flashbacks to driving over in the middle of the night and trying to navigate a parking spot as cars roared by, almost taking me and the driver's door with them. Our love never went beyond kissing and back rubbing. Even when I spent the night, it was cuddling and spooning in his boxers and Edie Sedgwick T-shirt. I mean, I knew deep down he was as gay as George Michael in a bathhouse listening to Cher, but I liked the idea of living atomic style with a South American who relished a nice Eames sofa and had an appreciation for melamine dishware.

As I cruised farther up the canyon, more film clips clicked through my mind. The afternoons I lay in bed with Michelle smoking Camel Lights and drinking ginger ale. Even now in our middle age we have been known to meet at my hotel, get under the covers, and consume a whole plate of chocolate chip cookies (the smoker's substitute) and ginger ale. Most of my Los Angeles days involved Michelle and ginger ale, Scrabble, cigarettes, and boys. Sometimes it was advice about a boy we were currently dating, sometimes about a boy we were trying to disengage from, and sometimes about boys from our adolescence. We were just young enough that the boys we had as teenagers could still surface for a do-over at any time. Now, they are all vague memories that resurface in dismal lives on Facebook.

But I liked the unpredictability of life then. Who would be the next love conquest? How could I juggle not two, but three men? My skin regimen consisted of soap and maybe astringent because I loved the Mediterranean blue color of the Kiehl's bottle. Now, my skin ritual takes an hour and requires the space of another bedroom for all the products. There are jars of antiaging, collagen-making, contouring, line-reducing, wrinkle-erasing creams scattered about my sink. And they will make me as nubile looking as rubbing a Hostess cupcake on my face will. But I have always been a victim of the promise.

I think that is why women my age seek affairs. They don't really love those men—the sexy father at baseball practice, the kid's guitar teacher, the thirty-year-old editor's assistant who makes fantastic cappuccinos. No, they want it all back. The sleepless nights overlooking the twinkling lights of Los Angeles with the possibility of a 3 A.M. burrito, a drive over to a blossoming romance, a skinny dip, or just knowing that the night holds no limits. I wonder what would happen if I got up one night now, checked on my sleeping children and snoring dogs, put on some jeans and black stiletto suede boots and whispered to my husband, "I'm going downtown to see what the city brings me"? I'm pretty sure it would not go over well; chances are, I would find myself stuck in a four-hour session with a psychopharmacologist the next day. I would definitely get a call from my mother.

That night in Los Angeles, I had some girlfriends, ghosts of the carefree past, over to dinner at the friend's house where I was staying—a perfectly manicured marble sculpture of a house ready for the pages of *Architectural Digest,* with nary a futon smelling of mold and stale beer in sight. I'd thought through the menu carefully. In-N-Out Burger was not an option, as all the girls were now watching their cholesterol, eating non-dairy (except for calcium supplements), and menopausally conscious of their caloric consumption. I made roast chicken, squash puree, and a standard for my lady set—kale salad. One thing that never changes is a girlfriend's yen for a cocktail; this is truly the single constant that never varies, from eighteen to eighty. I served my best tequila with ice and lots of lime. I had my usual club soda and cranberry juice. And very predictably, the ladies didn't eat much but sucked on their cocktails like they were connected to life support. And then the night got weird.

My friend Lucy began to discuss the inevitable wear and tear of her vagina. She has had four children and no amount of Pilates and Kegels in the world can sprinkle it with fairy dust and bring it back to its former pink rosebud state. "I think I have to do some work down there."

Katherine's eyes opened. "Like landscaping work?"

Lucy rolled her eyes. "No, plastic surgery. I don't

think I have stuff hanging down, but I want to get everything organized."

"But you're married. Who cares?" I whispered.

That might have been the end of it, if Peggy, the only lesbian in the group, hadn't had one too many tequilas and decided to egg Lucy on. "Well, let's see, we'll tell you!"

I had a moment of panic, hoping it wouldn't turn into some orgy—in which case I would have to coolly excuse myself to hide upstairs in my paisley pajamas with a mug of warm milk. And the Old Testament.

Lucy unbuttoned her purposely tattered and expensive jeans and lowered her La Perla underpants. It was the most finely trimmed and delicately pruned vagina I had ever seen. I knew Lucy would age well; she monitored every inch of her body like a guard at San Quentin. The rest of us sadly looked down at our vaginas, which we all knew looked like the back of *Grey Gardens*. In my youth I would have been best in show.

I decided on the plane ride home, in between episodes of *Downton Abbey,* that I was going to make an effort to infuse my life with more ebullience and adventure. But what exactly is my idea of excitement these days? A midnight bowl of fiber cereal while watching last Wednesday's *Law and Order SVU,* which is on too late to see it in real time? To quote Peggy Lee, "Is that all there is?" You see, I'm not ready for true adulthood! I don't want a colonoscopy! I don't wish to sleep with other people, but I would like a few men and perhaps a woman to at least try!

And whatever happens, I will not throw myself a big, blowout fiftieth birthday party. It would be like attending my own funeral, and then picking up the tab. I have been caught up in the flurry of fiftieth birthday parties and although I may dance like a soul sister until I'm covered in sweat and jump up and down like a sorority girl being handed carbs, it all makes me heartsick for sweet sixteen. These celebrations of the fact that we're still alive feel more like a segment of *This Is Your Life.* (Yes, I'm old enough to know that reference.) We all observe vintage childhood photos of the birthday girl carefully pasted on lavender boards and hanging about the room so we all can see just how deteriorated she has become.

How do I want to mark the fact that I will be turning half a century old? I want to fly to an island, alone, with a bag of books, no beauty creams, and a stash of Reese's Peanut Butter Cups. I want to dive in the ocean without worrying about how much cellulite I've acquired, like rings on a tree, or how, even from a distance, I would never be mistaken for a twenty-year-old. And when I dive into the sea where there are no sounds, I can just be. And I will marvel at the churning sand and the conch shells that are still perfect and pink even after decades of tumult. You see, underwater and above coral there are no TV executives, memories of Michelle and me buying a carton of Marlboro Lights at the 7-Eleven, old lovers, decaying bodies, Facebook, slide shows, or retrospective sadness. It's the only place where my vagina and I are ageless.

....

CHAPTER 22

Honkers If You Like

a Good Joke

I have never aspired to be a sex symbol. Or even sexy. In fact, I don't understand why the Phyllis Diller calendar hasn't sold as many as Marilyn Monroe's. I've always prided myself on the fact that my wit, not my tits, would get the man! Back when I was young (sniff sniff) and doing movies, I used to beg for a nudity clause. Not the typical nudity clause young ingenues would fight to put in because they refused to show their Lewinskis, but my own self-created one ensuring the production company that I would happily show my fun pillows at a mere ask.

I have an odd relationship with boobs. My mother claims I was breast-fed, but I have since concluded that because my parents divorced when I was one year old, I was likely bottle-fed by some random neighbor or the mean Eastern European lady that lived down the street, as my mother was understandably depressed at the time. So in my primary years we never got to solidify that maternal bond. Although I am fluent in Polish! But let's not dive into my own psychology (I have a team of specialists for that), or this story will take a sharp turn into a three-hundred-page book called "I'm Not OK, You're Not OK."

Suffice to say, breasts have no hold on me.

I completely get why women my age (post baby making) have boob jobs. Gravity and suckling take their toll and leave us with what can only be described as the real "deflategate." So I say cut them, sew them, glue them, duct-tape them . . . whatever you need to do to not burst into tears when entering the shower. I, however, am terrified of having a splinter removed, so I don't envision going under the knife anytime soon. Last spring I visited a friend who had just received breast augmentation (imagine Dolly Parton circa 1980) and was holed up in a hotel. She was packed in ice like a gift pack of steaks. After witnessing her wrapped in gauze and downing painkillers like popcorn at a matinee, I concluded I could never elect to put myself through the intense pain and recovery associated with a boob job. But the idea of room service is enticing.

Though of course if my husband leaves me for some juicy twenty-two-year-old Columbia Law student, you bet I'm spending my retirement fund on double Ds.

I was late for my call time at *Jimmy Kimmel Live*. It was my first time doing the show, and I was so excited and anxious about getting lost on Hollywood Boulevard that I momentarily took my eyes off the road and slammed into a hipster in a beaten and rusty Toyota Corolla. He had a ginger beard and strange piercings covering his lips. Before he could chastise me or call me a dumb bitch (something reserved for friends and family), I begged him for forgiveness, reassured him that I would take full responsibility, and pleaded for a swift conclusion as I was late for my guest slot on a popular late-night-TV talk show. I then pointed to the gigantic billboard of Jimmy Kimmel. He told me he was an aspiring (non-union) key grip. I promised I would put in a good word for him with Kimmel. After all, Los Angeles is the city of dreams.

When I called the cops to file a report I was asked if anyone was hurt. No. Anyone sexually assaulted? No. Then they hung up. What does a girl have to do to get arrested in that town?

I exchanged scribbles with the aspiring (nonunion) key grip and steered my dented, axle-challenged Hertz rental into a dilapidated parking lot surrounded by colorful graffiti. An eager producer met me and escorted me into the building. I was sweaty and spinning from the accident. Not the state I wanted to be in before performing on national TV.

I don't roll with an entourage. I mean, for goodness sake, I rented a car instead of accepting a limo and driver. Lesson learned. I usually show up with a paper bag containing a crumpled dress, my ID, and a breath mint. Joe, the show's hair-and-makeup guy, had meticulously displayed his foundations and eye shadows on the table and was pacing the room with a small plastic plate of stolen mini hot dogs from the greenroom. When I walked in I could practically read the bubble over his head: "Jesus, I can't fix this in ninety minutes!"

I threw down my bag and smelled my armpits. Joe dropped his plate in the trash. "Well, let's get started!" Makeup artists always like to ask what you're wearing. I suppose it's to match lipstick, but it instantly makes me insecure because I don't know the designer or haven't quite figured out what it is I am actually wearing and so can answer only, "I guess a black skirt."

Joe sprayed and teased. He painted on foundation and cover-up until I was as layered and spackled as one of those faux impressionist paintings you can buy in Central Park. (The magic of TV makeup is that while in real life you resemble the grandmother in some Showtime series, on HD television you look like Kate Bosworth.) Then I collapsed into the leather couch and watched Jimmy Kimmel do a skit mocking a Sia video. Joe came back into the room with his third plate of greenroom finger food and as many Snapples as he could carry. A young PA entered and updated us on the fact that the first guest was being delayed by Standards and Practices due to a wardrobe choice. So we waited another thirty minutes happily chomping on stuffed mushrooms. (Here's a tidbit most people don't know—the *Jimmy Kimmel* show serves fantastic hors d'oeuvres! So if you get a chance to book an appearance on the show, come hungry!

Finally the first guest entered the stage. Miley Cyrus. A girl/woman whose music or TV persona I knew only from my daughters' obsession with singing the *Hannah Montana* theme song and sticking their tongues out like overheated bassett hounds. Miley was the '80s Madonna on Red Bull and Pop Rocks. She wore two heart-shaped sequined pasties. Oh, and sequined pants. You gotta leave something to the imagination. Of course Joe spat out some hummus. "Oh my God, what is she *wearing*?" Well, she's in the music business and probably needs to stand out. And that's being kind. But who was I to judge, sitting cross-legged in a black knee-length skirt and sensible Chloe cream blouse?

Now, had Miley not commented on her wardrobe, perhaps the evening would have ended differently. But I could have sworn she was looking in my direction as she bragged about how "her boobs were really good" and how much she loved her boobs—topped by "I mean, when I'm older and saggy I'm not going to do this!"

I had just smeared my mini hot dog in spicy mustard. "Oh Lord," I barked out loud.

"Right?" said Joe.

"No, I mean, I have to . . ." I ran to the door and beckoned over a PA. "Listen, can you go to wardrobe and ask them if they have any pasties like the ones Miley is wearing? There has to be backup."

The PA stared at me like I just tied a cherry stem in a knot with my tongue. "But you're on in five minutes!"

"I know, I know. Can you just see?"

Suddenly, a producer came flying into room with flop sweat and bulging eyes. "What's going on? What do you need?"

I braced my arms on his shoulders, "I need pasties, and I'm going out in them!" The producer started jumping up and down like he won the dining room set on *The Price Is Right*! And off he sprinted. He knew whatever it was I was thinking it was provocative, and provocative meant ratings and Twitter trending. Nobody wants the Nobel Peace Prize or Pulitzer anymore; the greatest achievement is to go viral. If I had asked for a bucket of Vaseline and a donkey I would have gotten the same response.

Joe, wide-eyed, inquired, "Um, what are you doing?"

"I'm going to show Miley Cyrus that older women with saggy tatas can also wear pasties!" He grabbed my plate and scarfed my mini hot dog. I think he ate part of the fork.

There was a knock and in flew a rather robust sound guy, the PA, and another semiofficial dude whose job still escapes me. I'm not even sure if he even worked there. It was like a scene from *Broadcast News*—people shoving each other out of the way, the sound guy sweating profusely trying to figure out where to hide the battery pack, and the wardrobe people who rather aggressively smashed the sequined pasties on my boobsters. A panicked PA yelled, "Two minutes! She's on in two minutes!"

"Let's hope they don't fall off," the sound guy muttered under his breath.

Joe was hiding behind a potted plant with some bite-size brownies. He didn't want any part of the catastrophe that was about to transpire. In my goody bag, I found a *Jimmy Kimmel* sweatshirt—bingo. I wouldn't have to spend the whole interview looking like an aged cocktail waitress at an assisted-living Hooters.

I walked down the hallway toward the stage, praying that my comedic instincts had not served me wrong. Suddenly I was face-to-face (or titties-to-titties) with Miley. Other half-naked youngsters and publicists and security guards flanked her. I flashed her my milkshakes and she smiled her toothy smile. "That's fucking excellent!" And she thrust out hers. I finally understood the slang term "bumping uglies."

Then came the moment of reckoning. I was escorted behind the stage entrance door. You know, the place where celebrities awkwardly dance the long stretch from the door to the host and the desk. I heard Jimmy announce, "Please welcome Ali Wentworth!" I turned the knob, opened the door, and held my breath. My *Kimmel* sweatshirt was zipped up to my chin. I walked with confidence toward him, gave him a hug, turned to the audience, and unzipped my sweatshirt. I counted to three and zipped it back up.

I was ready for anything: the "ewws" of disgust, rotten okra thrown at my head, or audience members standing up and walking out in protest. It was a live show. There was no turning back. To my relief, I heard laughter, clapping, and some seallike barking. I hadn't been obscene, I told myself (well, except in the eyes of the Orthodox community and possibly my fourth-grade math teacher, Ms. Fletcher), and the rest of the segment was supported with funny stories from my book so the focus wasn't only on my rib bumpers. As I walked off the stage, though, my only thought was that I had to e-mail my husband and explain everything before he got side-slapped with bits and pieces of "your wife" and "topless." For a wife who lives in perpetual fear of embarrassing her husband, this latest stunt had not been the wisest gamble, perhaps. I might have to spend the rest of our marriage in a kennel cage.

Jimmy Kimmel had beaten me to it with a one-line e-mail to George: "Comedy demanded it!" What a class act! I gave him my front and he had my back.

The next morning my eyes flickered open at around 5 A.M. The sun wasn't up, but my cell phone was. I could see the mass of flashing texts. I hesitated. Probably the same way Custer did in his last stand, not that he knew for sure he would be massacred. All I needed from the universe was acknowledgement and reassurance of a joke well executed. I was not looking for compliments on my body, my boobs, or placement of pasties. But, ironically, that's what I got. A text from my twelve-year-old daughter read, "Mom, *E! News* says you're hotter than Miley Cyrus!" My husband commented that my "working out was paying off." *Wait a minute!* What about funny? What about the cleverness involved, the lightning-speed wit?

(My sister was, reliably, the lone dissenter. She e-mailed a screenshot of me and my pasties, along with the comment, "Do you know about this???!!!!??" That

"???!!!!??" spoke volumes. "Yes," I answered. "I know about it because that's me!" Did she think I was sleep stripping?)

As the day progressed, the back-patting continued. "You're trending on Twitter," my daughter proudly sang into the phone. It was out of control. My daughters were absorbing the wrong message. They would grow up and forgo Yale for the Playboy mansion! I could see the bumper sticker: if you show your boobs, good things will happen! I countered with diagrams, charts, and *The Feminine Mystique* until they finally got that it was a joke and not my new way of life.

There are two opinions that I rely on in my life: my husband's and my mother's. I had been relieved to discover that George thought the show was hilarious. I waited to hear from my mother. It felt like those old black-and-white 1940s films when the calendar pages rapidly fly off one by one while simultaneously the arms of a clock accelerate as they rotate.

And finally the e-mail came in: "If you had to flash you did it with grace and charm. Now . . . come home and put on the apron right way front and get back to reality!"

Quite right.

ACKNOWLEDGMENTS

I would like to acknowledge my editor, Jennifer Barth. In fact, this book should be dedicated to her. I tried many times to give back my advance because I was consumed with children and chronic head colds. She would not accept and pleaded with me to keep writing. When I was at the end of my rope, my brain throbbing from spellcheck, Jennifer would still meet me for lunch. And pay.

Last summer I was bedridden with pneumonia and wanted to postpone my book. Jennifer warmly convinced me that delirium was a form of creativity. When I cut my leg open and received sixty stitches . . . well, you can guess—she encouraged me to keep writing. With my leg propped up. And drugged out.

There would not be a book, let alone an acknowledgments page, without the insistence, encouragement, and support of Jennifer Barth. I more than acknowledge her; I bow to her.

(Jennifer Barth did not edit this page.)

I would also like to thank HarperCollins for all their ongoing support and creative input.

And Daisy, my obese dachshund, who showed the whole crew at the book-cover photo shoot what a true diva is!

ABOUT THE AUTHOR

....

ALI WENTWORTH is the author of the *New York Times* bestseller *Ali in Wonderland*. She made a name for herself on the comedy show *In Living Color* and has appeared on such television shows as *The Tonight Show with Jay Leno*, *Seinfeld*, *Head Case*, and *The Oprah Winfrey Show*, for which she was a correspondent. Her film credits include *Jerry Maguire*, *The Real Blonde*, *Office Space*, and *It's Complicated*. A native of Washington, D.C., she lives in New York City with her husband, George Stephanopoulos, and their two girls.

ALSO BY *NEW YORK TIMES* BESTSELLING AUTHOR
ALI WENTWORTH

ALI IN WONDERLAND
And Other Tall Tales

Growing up in a family of political journalists—and daughter of President Reagan's White House social secretary—Ali Wentworth rebelled against her blue-blood upbringing, embracing Hollywood, motorcycles, even a few wildly inappropriate marriage proposals. Today she is an acclaimed comedic actress and writer, former Oprah regular, wife of political and media star George Stephanopoulos, and a mother who lets her two girls eat cotton candy before bed. In this addictively funny and warm memoir, she takes us through the looking glass and into the wonderland of her life, from a childhood among Washington's elite to a stint in the psych ward they called a New England prep school; days doing L.A. sketch comedy (with then-aspiring artists Will Ferrell and Lisa Kudrow) to a series of spectacularly failed loves (that eventually led her to Mr. Right).